FLAVOURS FROM THE **FINNISH** COUNTRYSIDE

MARKUS MAULAVIRTA   SEBASTIAN NURMI   CHRISTER LINDGREN

FLAVOURS FROM THE **FINNISH** COUNTRYSIDE

First published in Finnish under the title
Mestari Markuksen ruokamatka

© The authors and
Otava Publishing Company 2005
Photographs by Sebastian Nurmi
Layout by Nina Laine
English translation by Malcolm Hicks

Printed by
Otava Book Printing Ltd
Keuruu, Finland, 2006

ISBN-13: 978-951-1-21123-5
ISBN-10: 951-1-21123-4

CONTENTS

FOREWORD 7

IN MARKUS' OPINION 8

GREEN VEGETABLES
BESIDE THE ASPARAGUS
PATCH 13

ROOT VEGETABLES
ENJOY THE FRUITS
OF THE EARTH 28

FISH
AT LEAST TWICE A WEEK 43

MEAT
THE REVIVAL OF
FLAVOURSOME PORK 71

LAMB
FINNISH SHEEP ARE
THE REAL THING! 85

POULTRY
DELICIOUS POULTRY! 94

REINDEER
REINDEER BREEDING
IS AN ART! 108

CHEESE
IS FINLAND BECOMING
A LAND OF CHEESE? 123

BREAD
EVERY LOAF OF BREAD IS
WORTH A SONG 130

WINE
WINE FROM FINLAND?
OF COURSE. 141

BEER
LET'S HAVE A QUICK BEER 144

DESSERTS
FLAVOURS, FIBRES AND
FLAVONOIDS 147

THE STARS OF THIS BOOK 162

INDEX 164

THANKS 166

FOREWORD

Our food is part of our culture, and small, local producers lie at the heart of this food culture. They represent an alternative that we would do well to favour. The aim of this book is to encourage those who appreciate good food to look around them, at what is available close at hand, and to find new, exciting flavours in the places where they live. We also want to motivate small producers and entrepreneurs and encourage them to continue in their endeavours, in which they will find that they have the support of an increasing number of people who enjoy good food.

Flavours from the Finnish Countryside takes the form of a journey through Finland from south to north, from the potato fields to the grazing grounds of the reindeer. On the way we will meet small country producers and processors of foodstuffs who have been discovered by the master chef Markus Maulavirta in the course of his restaurant work. These are in effect the main characters in our story, actors who are united by a common striving for high quality.

The book contains about sixty of Maulavirta's favourite recipes, most of which are easy to prepare at home. Some of the ingredients may be difficult to obtain outside Finland, but we trust that readers will be able to make use of local equivalents, or of substitutes that are more generally available in supermarkets, for instance. The important thing is to relax and adapt the recipes to your own needs, to improvise and enjoy this straightforward, uncomplicated attitude to cooking. Explorations in the little shops, farm outlets and local markets of your own home area are always worthwhile. You will never guess what delicacies might be waiting for you there, just round the corner! There are many valuable and tasty dishes and ingredients that we have not been able to mention in this book, of course, and where we mention particular Finnish growers and suppliers of foodstuffs we naturally assume that readers elsewhere will be able to find local producers of equal merit in their own areas and will come to appreciate them in the same way.

We have set out from the beginning to write a book that is easy to read and easy to use. We have tried not to preach, although the endless restrictions and unfathomable rules and bureaucracy that afflict small producers of foodstuffs nowadays could easily have tempted us to do so. Perhaps the best way to advance the cause of wholesome, local country food, however, is simply to enjoy Markus Maulavirta's recipes and the short comments that come with them.

The recipes are intended for 4–5 persons unless otherwise stated.

Markus Maulavirta
Sebastian Nurmi
Christer Lindgren

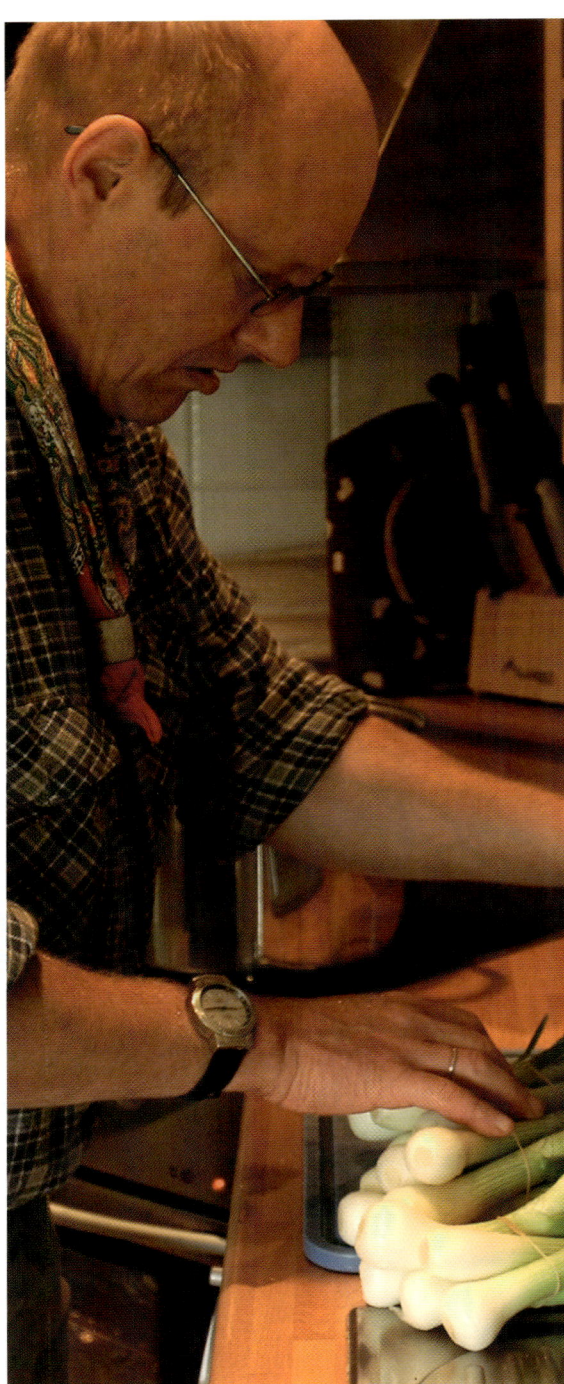

IN MARKUS' OPINION

SHOULD WE PREFER FINNISH FOOD?

As Finns, of course we should. When we buy Finnish food we are providing employment for Finnish producers, processors and small entrepreneurs. It would be ridiculous, though, to base our food shopping and restaurant meals entirely on the state of the national economy, as many of us are operating on a tight budget and these are not questions of charity. In the end we have to try to find good things for our table at reasonable prices, but we should prefer Finnish food whenever it is reasonable to do so.

We Finns nevertheless easily fail to see the good things that are on offer on our very doorstep. I constantly hear and see foreign visitors to our restaurant remarking on the fresh, tasty Finnish fish and vegetables that we serve, and the berry wines from small country wineries often prove more than acceptable to people from France and other major wine-producing areas, who are eager to ask about them and discuss them. What sort of inferiority complex are we suffering from?

THE FINNISH FOOD CULTURE

At last we are beginning to realize in Finland that food is a part of our culture, and thus a part of our national identity. What we need now is deeds on the part of the government authorities to match their words: a medal or two and an invitation to the president's Independence Day reception would be a good start, but above all a purposeful effort to project Finland as a gastronomic nation – backed up, of course, by the necessary financial input.

The Finnish food culture is at the same time global, of course. Styles and influences, ingredients and professional cooks all move effortlessly across national boundaries these days. On the other hand, without its own flavours, tastes, producers, styles and specialities Finland would very soon disappear from the gastronomic map.

Viewed from one perspective, our food culture represents a tradition that should be preserved. Up to now this has been the prerogative of a small group of dedicated professionals in the restaurant and catering business. On the other hand, it also involves a new, creative, youthful culture which, while firmly rooted in tradition, is prepared to follow the spirit of the times and march bravely into the future. This aspect of our gastronomic scene deserves especial support.

And what is the Finns' national dish? Some would say Spaghetti Bolognese. There you have it! Is it time to take up arms on behalf of Finnish food?

LOCAL PRODUCE

Small-scale producers lie at the heart of the food culture of every geographical area, and these producers are normally local ones, if only because a small-scale operator cannot usually aspire to a distribution and marketing network that covers the whole country.

It is precisely in this sense that local produce offers the finest alternative of all. Wherever you may travel in Finland, you will always find a local bakery close at hand whose bread, whether flat, unleavened barley bread or dark loaves of rye bread, will have a distinctive taste of its own and as such will be by far the best thing to try. If you are lucky you may find a fish stall at the local market place which has perch that were still swimming in a nearby lake the evening before. You will also find personifications of the fine flavours and quality produce of the area, in that you may meet the bakers, fishermen, vegetable growers etc. in person.

The greatest thing of all about local produce, however, is that it is fresh. Your lettuce will have been picked by a caring hand early that morning, perhaps only a few hours ago, with the dew still on it, and the joint of local pork may have been from an animal slaughtered in the same week, so that it has never seen the inside of a deep-freeze.

Is it not worth paying a euro or two extra for fresh, high quality delicacies from small, local producers?

FRESHNESS RECONSIDERED

Although an unbroken cold-storage chain is an established virtue which nobody is prepared to forsake nowadays, it does not necessarily guarantee freshness. A cold-storage chain can operate efficiently between Bangkok and Helsinki, for instance, but you still don't know when your king prawns were fished out of the sea or where they were stored before starting out on their fast, cold journey to Finland. In the same way, you don't know at what age your fillet of salmon was sealed in its vacuum pack with the "Best before" date stamped on it. Ask, and insist on an answer. You will get better food that way.

TRACEABILITY

When a loaf of rye bread made from refreshed leaven at a small bakery in Kemiö was awarded the prize for the best food product in Finland at the Gastro Food Fair in spring 2004, one interesting aspect was that every stage in its production could be traced precisely. We had bought it from the small bakery café next to the local filling station, and the flour for it had come from a mill a couple of kilometres away that received its grain from a maximum distance of 20 kilometres, from a known farmer who could have pointed to the precise strip of field where the rye was grown. The bread was still warm as we drove from Kemiö to Helsinki, and the authentic country butter from the Jukkola dairy that we spread on it was bought from our trusted supplier, the "Flying Cow" dairy stall in Hakaniemi Market Hall, which stocks a wide variety of cheeses from small country dairies and excellent traditional hand-churned butter.

Our restaurant clients take great delight time and again in such stories of the production chains on which the particular flavours of the dishes they enjoy actually depend.

MORE SMALL MARKETS!

The best places to find delicious food from small, local producers are direct farm outlets and various country markets. Even the smallest of producers are able to bring their wares to these, and they are often frequented by summer residents of the country areas and knowledgeable passers-by. Small, private shops and stalls in the market halls and open markets of larger towns and cities also represent the same production and service culture. Personal service, information on the products on sale and responsibility for their quality are things that it is worth paying a little extra for.

It is also worth asking about local products at your own food shop. If people ask often enough, it is quite likely that some local products will appear on the shelves and in the window displays.

COMMITMENT AND DEDICATION

The factor uniting all the producers and processors of foodstuffs on whose work this book is based is their commitment to their own line of production and to the achieving of high standards. Quality is the only real area in which small producers can be competitive.

Fundamentally, quality depends entirely on the producer. My lettuce supplier, *Ville Holopainen,* is a good example of this sense of responsibility. If a lettuce isn't good enough by his quality criteria, it won't be good enough for me, so it goes onto the compost heap and he resolves to try better next time.

THE QUALITY CHAIN IS A SERIOUS MATTER

By international standards, and in the face of massive imports of foodstuffs, the whole of Finnish food production is in effect small-scale and local. In other words, it is quality that counts! In this sense the Quality Chain project coordinated by the Ministry of Agriculture and Forestry is a serious matter, its main purpose being to induce all those involved in the food production chain to commit themselves to mutually agreed standards. In practice this means that farmers agree to use only approved seed, fodder and fertilizers, that animals are looked after in an acceptable manner and that due attention is paid to environmental questions connected with food production. Similarly, care is taken that the cold-storage chain functions smoothly, so that the produce reaches the shops or restaurants in prime condition, with its freshness and flavour preserved.

It is important, of course, that the same chain is continued in the shops and restaurants themselves, so that quality is maintained "from the field to the plate", as it should be. And it must be remembered that good table service is also a quality factor.

Training, advice and supervision are constantly required, and public relations and the provision of information are also important. The shopper or restaurant guest has a right to know where the fish was last swimming or where the potatoes were grown, when they left these places and when they arrived, ready to be enjoyed by the customer.

Quality is flavour.
Quality is good food.

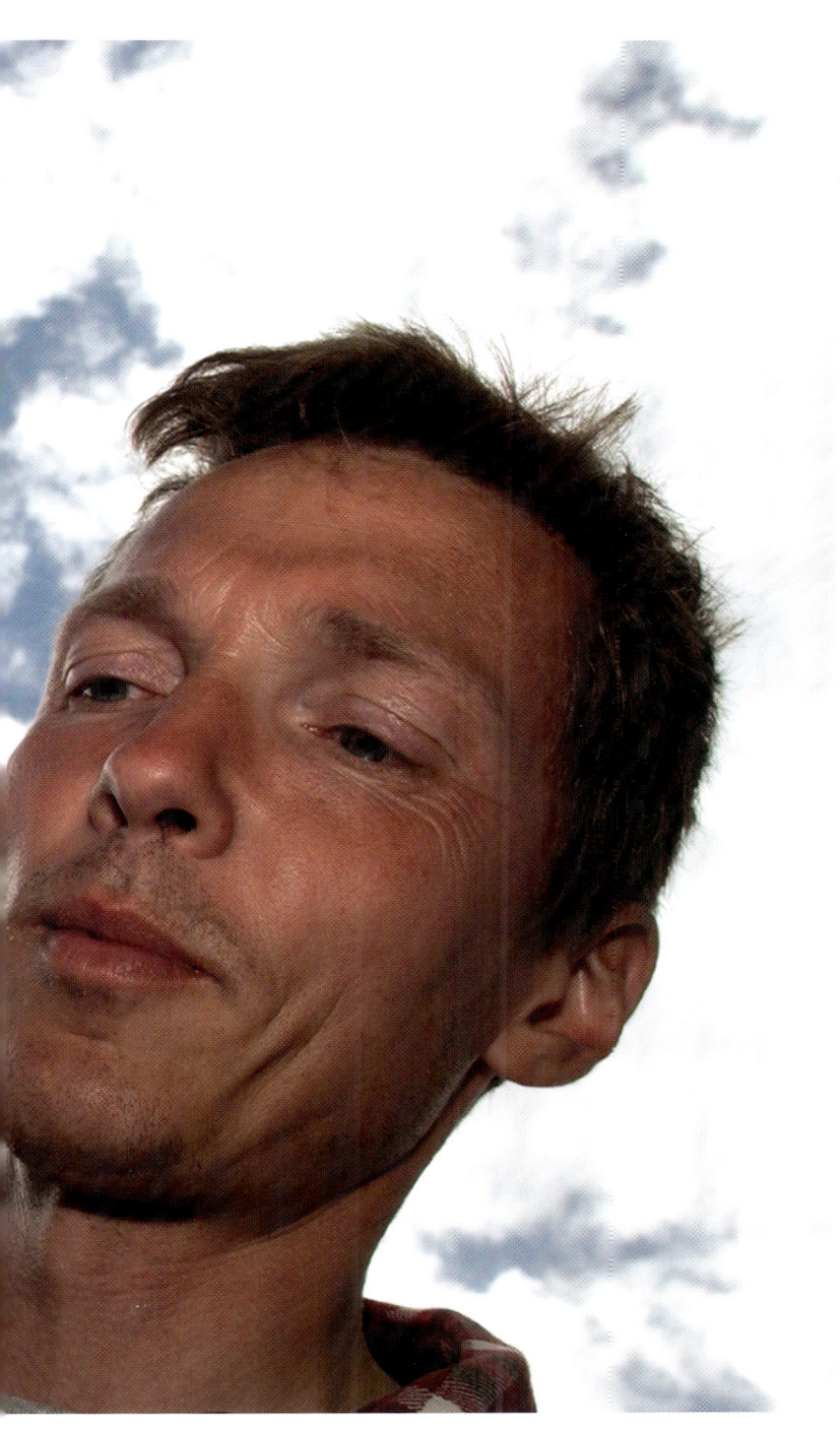

BESIDE THE ASPARAGUS PATCH

Finnish vegetables are the best example of how freshness, cleanness and care and attention from the grower can affect flavour and quality. The growing season in Finland is short but intensive, as there is an abundance of light. You can taste this in the vegetables.

For the strawberry grower *Magnus Koskinen,* spring is the time for asparagus. There are already a number of people growing green asparagus in Finland, and white asparagus is known to have been cultivated on the Paddainen estate since the 1920s.

This refined spring delicacy in fact manages well at Finnish latitudes. There are some problems with weeds and night frosts, but there are also advantages, such as the nutrient-rich soil and the clean air. And perhaps most important for us, the produce reaches us fresh. "We usually pick the asparagus early in the morning and deliver it to our customers immediately, at a temperature of two degrees. This uninterrupted cold chain is especially important with asparagus," Magnus Koskinen explains.

Ville Holopainen, on his family farm in Kirkkonummi, picks his lettuces early in the morning as well, as they are at their freshest after a cool night.

"Spring onions that have been grown to a length of 10 or 15 cm and washed after picking can be tossed straight into the pan," he maintains. "Our cooperation with Markus has helped us develop our products and put more effort into quality. If something doesn't come up to our own standards it goes straight on the compost heap," he claims.

THERE IS OFTEN SOME SOIL BETWEEN THE LAYERS OF A LEEK. CUT THE STEM LENGTHWAYS UP TO ABOUT HALF ITS HEIGHT AND RINSE WITH WARM WATER.

ASPARAGUS RAISED FROM SEED WILL GIVE ITS FIRST HARVEST AFTER 3 OR 4 YEARS, BUT IF RAISED FROM PLANTS IT WILL REACH THIS STAGE THE FOLLOWING YEAR. GREEN ASPARAGUS GROWS ON THE SURFACE OF THE SOIL AND WHITE ENTIRELY UNDERGROUND. THE BEST SOIL IS A SANDY MULL.

ALTHOUGH HOLOPAINEN'S LETTUCES ARE CLEANED AS SOON AS THEY ARE PICKED, THEY ARE GIVEN A FINAL WASH IN COLD WATER IN THE RESTAURANT'S KITCHENS, SO THAT THEY WILL BE FRESH WHEN THEY COME TO THE TABLE AND WILL LAST LONGER.

THEIR HIGH WATER CONTENT MAKES CUCUMBERS VERY SUSCEPTIBLE TO TEMPERATURE VARIATIONS. THE BEST TEMPERATURE TO STORE THEM AT IS ABOUT 10–14°C. FINNISH CUCUMBERS DON'T NEED TO BE PEELED BEFORE USE.

FRESH ASPARAGUS KEEPS WELL IF WRAPPED IN COLD, DAMP KITCHEN PAPER OR TOWELLING, PREFERABLY IN AN UPRIGHT POSITION. TRANSFER IT TO A BOWL WITH A COUPLE OF CENTIMETRES OF WATER AT THE BOTTOM, STILL STANDING UPRIGHT, ABOUT TWO HOURS BEFORE SERVING.

THE THIN SKIN ON FRESH GREEN ASPARAGUS ONLY NEEDS TO BE PEELED VERY LIGHTLY, BUT THE MORE FIBROUS SKIN ON WHITE ASPARAGUS NEEDS MORE THOROUGH PEELING. CUT THE DRY BUTT AWAY FIRST AND THEN PEEL OFF WHOLE STRIPS WITH A SHARP POTATO PEELER, STARTING A CENTIMETRE OR SO BELOW THE TIP. TAKE EACH STRIP OUT OF THE PEELER BEFORE TURNING THE ASPARAGUS SLIGHTLY AND REPEATING THE SAME MOVEMENT.

CUCUMBER AND WHITEFISH ROE IN SORREL SAUCE

1/2–1 fresh cucumber

salt

black pepper from a mill

2–3 dl whipping cream

3–5 tbsp white currant wine or ordinary white wine

3 tbsp chopped parsley

2–3 leaves of sorrel

100–150 g whitefish roe

a small piece of toasted bread for each person

Peel the cucumber, cut it in half lengthways and gouge out the seeds with a spoon. Cut the halves lengthways into halves again and season with salt and pepper. Add the cream and wine. Cook on the stove or in a 200°C oven for 5–7 mins. Take the cucumber slices out of the liquid and add the finely chopped parsley and sorrel.

Place the cucumbers on a serving plate. Cook the sauce for a moment and pour it over the cucumbers. Arrange the roe on the pieces of toast and serve along with the cucumber.

Fresh cucumber can be used for other things as well as salads or slicing onto bread. The sorrel for this dish was from Ville Holopainen's market garden. If unobtainable, it can be replaced with chives or omitted entirely.

LEEKS AU GRATIN, WITH GOAT CHEESE SAUCE

4–6 leeks

Cut the leeks in half lengthways up to half their height and rinse them in warm water to remove any soil or sand. Then cut them into pieces about 10 cm long (three pieces per leek). Cook them in a large quantity of salt water for 3–4 mins, then transfer them to cold water or rinse them carefully in cold running water to stop them cooking. Place them on a cloth or piece of kitchen paper to dry.

SAUCE:

45 g butter

45 g plain flour

1.5 dl cream

3.5 dl full-fat milk

grated nutmeg

salt and black pepper from a mill

150–200 g grated goat's milk gruyere cheese

Melt the butter in a pan on the stove and add the flour. Allow the flour to swell for a moment and then add the cold cream and milk and stir well so that the liquid begins to thicken to a sauce as it heats up. Continue stirring vigorously to remove any lumps from the sauce. Simmer for 7–10 mins, season and add 2/3 of the grated cheese.

Spread a couple of tablespoonfuls of sauce on the bottom of a greased oven dish and arrange the leeks in a row on top of this. Pour the rest of the sauce onto the leeks and sprinkle with the remaining grated cheese. Bake in a 225°C oven for about 15 mins or until the sauce begins to brown.

You can also use this cheese sauce on fried mushrooms, or pieces of fried smoked ham, or both.

In classic French cuisine vegetables are usually rinsed with cold water after boiling in order to stop the cooking process. Here it stops the leeks from cooking any further and helps to preserve their beautiful colour.

The goat's milk gruyere that I use for this dish is produced by the Juustoportti Dairy and is one of the strongest of the Finnish goat cheeses.

ASPARAGUS MARINADED IN ORANGE OIL, WITH VIRGIN SALAD

5–8 sticks of fresh asparagus
1 dl rapeseed oil
juice of half an orange
1 sprig of fresh thyme
2 slices of orange peel
2 tbsp sunflower seeds

Bring the peeled asparagus to the boil in salt water and allow to cool. Place the sticks together with the herbs and orange peel in a mixture of the oil and orange juice. Roast the sunflower seeds in a dry pan with no oil and sprinkle them onto the asparagus. Serve with a fresh salad.

ASPARAGUS SALAD WITH OVEN-DRIED TOMATOES

20–30 sticks of fresh green asparagus

4 tomatoes
1 sprig of fresh rosemary
2 sprigs of fresh thyme
black pepper from a mill
salt from a salt-cellar or mill
1–2 cloves of garlic
0.5 dl virgin rapeseed oil

a variety of lettuces
lemon juice to taste

Cut the tomatoes in half and remove their stalks. Sprinkle the exposed surfaces with finely chopped rosemary and thyme and season with salt and pepper. Place the tomatoes on an oven tray, cut surface upwards, and dry them in the oven for 6–7 hours at 80°C.

Chop the garlic into small pieces and stir these into the oil. Sprinkle drops of oil onto the tomatoes. Peel the asparagus carefully with a potato peeler, always working from the top down to the base, so that no long, hard fibres are left on the surface. Cook in water with plenty of salt for 5 – 8 mins depending on the thickness of the sticks. Cool under running cold water and drain.

Wash the lettuce and tear into pieces, season with rapeseed oil, lemon juice, black pepper and salt. Add the tomatoes and asparagus and serve.

The drying time can be extended to 8–10 hours by setting the oven temperature at 70°C. Put the tomatoes in the oven the night before and take them out in the morning.

ASPARAGUS, COUNTRY BUTTER SAUCE AND BELLY OF PORK

COUNTRY BUTTER SAUCE:

6 egg yolks

300 g country butter

juice of 1 lemon

cayenne pepper

(salt)

STOCK:

3 tbsp white wine vinegar

2 dl dry green currant wine or dry white wine

3–4 tbsp finely chopped onion

10 white peppers, crushed

1 bay leaf

a couple of sprigs of parsley

First prepare the stock. Heat a saucepan and pour in the white wine vinegar. There will be a little splutter and the vinegar will soften nicely in taste. Add the wine, onion and herbs and reduce the stock to about 0.5 dl. This will concentrate its flavour.

Put the egg yolks into a round-bottomed bowl and strain the reduced stock on top of them. The bowl should be larger in diameter than the saucepan intended for steaming.

Pour 2–3 dl of water into the saucepan, depending on the size of the bowl, and bring it to the boil. Then place the bowl on top of the pan of boiling water and heat the mixture while beating it vigorously. Be careful: the mixture will cook surprisingly quickly.

When the mixture has become a firm froth and no longer tastes of raw egg, take the bowl off the saucepan and gradually add knobs of butter that have been softened at room temperature. Finally season with lemon juice and a pinch of cayenne pepper. Add salt if necessary.

ASPARAGUS:

5–10 sticks of peeled white or green asparagus per person

a piece of smoked belly of pork

Peel the asparagus "twice over" with a potato peeler to make sure that none of the outside skin remains. Cook the sticks in salt water for 3–8 mins depending on their thickness. Asparagus is done if it droops slightly when you hold the stick in the middle.

Cut the pork into suitably sized slices and fry them in their own fat. Serve the asparagus with a slice of pork and a generous spoonful of country butter sauce.

CHANTERELLES, POACHED EGG AND BELLY OF PORK

fresh chanterelles, ceps, horns of plenty or other suitable wild mushrooms that can be used without blanching

1 medium-sized onion

butter for frying

(1 tsp plain flour)

5–7 dl whipping cream

1 tbsp soy sauce

black pepper from a mill

salt

4–8 slices smoked belly of pork or ham

Clean the mushrooms and cut them into fairly big pieces. Finely chop the onion.

Heat a frying pan well and fry the mushroom pieces in butter. Add the onion and fry for a moment longer. Sprinkle a teaspoonful of flour on top of the mushrooms if desired. Stir well and add the cream. Allow to simmer until the sauce has reached a suitable thickness. Season with soy sauce, pepper and salt.

POACHED EGGS:

1 litre hot water

0.5 dl spirit vinegar

a little salt

4 free-range eggs

Bring the water to the boil, add the vinegar and salt and allow to bubble for a while. Break the eggs one at a time into a cup and lower the cup gently to the surface before tipping the egg sharply into the water. Allow the egg to stay in the water for a few minutes, until cooked, and then scoop it out with a draining spoon. Place the poached eggs on a piece of kitchen paper to dry.

Fry the slices of pork in their own fat and serve them out with the mushrooms. Place a poached egg on top of each portion. Serve with boiled rice if you wish.

High-quality pork fed on cereal will not sputter in the pan nearly as much as belly of pork usually does.

ENJOY THE FRUITS OF THE EARTH

Potatoes, young beetroots, carrots, turnips and other familiar root vegetables are tasty, healthy and cheap all the year round, and the new enthusiasm being shown for these vegetables in Finland, even in restaurants, is a wonderful thing.

There are some places in the world where swedes are only fed to animals, but then those that grow there are rather woody and tasteless. Our sweet-tasting swedes and small, delicious turnips, like those still grown in clearings made by burning the forest, in some places in Lieksa in the east of Finland, for example, have a marvellous taste. The abundance of nutrients in the soil obviously makes all the difference!

Juhani Hirvonen, a farmer at Ylämylly in Liperi, has been selling potatoes in the local market since he was ten years old. He took up full-time farming 30 years ago and is now growing Asterix, Van Gogh and other strains of potato that are popular in Finland. His main aim is to achieve the highest possible quality, which means choosing suitable strains for the local conditions, applying a mild fertilizer and watering the crop to just the right extent. His latest project is to try to bring the traditional black potatoes back into the shops. "It's all for the benefit of the customer," he maintains.

For Juha Hirvonen potato growing is a calling in life and an object of continual experimentation and product development, although it is often something of a sparring match with other growers. He is convinced, however, that the quality of Finnish potatoes has improved in recent years, and is pleased that useful training in potato growing is available nowadays.

Try buying your potatoes at a farm outlet or country market. All root vegetables are at their best when they still have their soil on them. Once washed, even if covered in soil again for appearances, potatoes will be impossible to clean just by brushing and will have to be peeled.

NEW POTATOES, VENDACE ROE AND DILL IN SMETANA

a suitable amount of new potatoes
plain flour for coating the potatoes
salt
pepper
a mixture of butter and rapeseed oil for frying

Boil the potatoes, cool them down and cut them into thickish slices. Mix the flour, salt and pepper, and coat the potatoes on both sides. Fry them in the mixture of butter and rapeseed oil until crisp.

DILL IN SMETANA:
2 tbsp milk
a bunch of finely chopped dill
2 dl smetana
salt
pepper

vendace roe

Mix the milk and dill in a liquidizer and add the smetana a moment later. The sauce should be a beautiful green in colour. Season judiciously with salt and pepper.

Place the potatoes on a plate with the sauce and vendace roe beside them.

POTATO PANCAKE AND HERRING CAVIAR

300 g Rosamunda potatoes

4 dl milk

3 egg yolks

3 tbsp flour

100 g melted butter

salt

grated nutmeg

fresh ground black pepper

3 egg whites

butter for frying

Cook, peel and mash the potatoes. Add the milk, egg yolks, flour and melted butter. Season the pancake batter with salt, nutmeg and pepper. Beat the egg white to a firm froth and add to the batter. Frying in butter in a pan for individual pancakes.

HERRING CAVIAR:

2 fillets of Matjes herring

10 cm fresh cucumber

1 pickled cucumber

1 cooking apple

chives or the stem of a spring onion

2 tbsp capers

white pepper

fish roe

Cut all the ingredients into small cubes, mix them together and season with pepper. It is not essential to peel the cucumbers for this. Form the herring caviar into a cake with a small can or yoghurt pot opened at both ends and place this partly on top of the pancake. Garnish with a spoonful of roe.

HIRVONEN'S BLACK POTATOES

600 g small black potatoes, washed
1 kg coarse salt

SOUR CREAM SAUCE:

2 dl crème fraîche or the creamy variety of the Finnish fermented milk product viili
0.5 dl balsámico wine vinegar
a bunch of parsley and chives, finely chopped
4 tbsp liquid honey
black pepper from a mill

Cook the potatoes in the coarse salt in a 220°C oven for about an hour. You can either bury them in salt, which will make them crisp on the outside, or place them on a bed of salt and sprinkle a little over them. I prefer burying them entirely.

Mix all the sauce ingredients together a few hours before serving.

Cut the potatoes in half while still warm, place them on a bed of lettuce leaves, e.g. Rucola lettuce, and serve with the cream sauce.

Black potatoes are one traditional variety that Juhani Hirvonen has been trying to re-introduce. A limited quantity was on sale in autumn 2005.

Save the salt for cooking another batch of potatoes – or for melting the ice on your garden path.

BEETROOTS BAKED IN THE OVEN, WITH GOAT CHEESE SAUCE

4 fresh beetroots, all of a similar size
4 pieces of aluminium foil
rapeseed oil for greasing

a quantity of small-leafed virgin lettuce

Wrap the whole, unpeeled beetroots in greased foil and bake them in a 220°C oven for about an hour or until they are cooked. Cool them and peel them.

GOAT CHEESE SAUCE:
100 g soft goat's milk cheese
3 tbsp honey
4–5 tbsp wine vinegar
freshly ground black pepper
salt
1 dl rapeseed oil

Take the rind off the cheese and put all the ingredients together in a liquidizer. Reduce to a fine pulp and add enough oil to make a suitably thick sauce.

Wash the lettuce and arrange it on the plates with segments of beetroot. Add the sauce and serve with the herb-flavoured savoury form of comb pastries (see p. 139).

The Finnish Niittymaa fresh goat cheese is my favourite for this dish, but you can equally well use any other soft chèvre-type cheese.

BEETROOT TIMBALE WITH LINGONBERRY SAUCE AND CEPS

4 fresh medium-sized beetroots
1 tbsp rapeseed oil
1/2–1 finely chopped onion
3 tbsp red wine vinegar
2–3 dl smetana
3 eggs
grated nutmeg
black pepper from mill
salt

Peel the beetroots and cut them into thumbnail-sized pieces. Heat the oil and lightly fry the pieces of beetroot and onion in it for a few minutes. Add the vinegar and smetana and allow to simmer for about ten minutes.

Reduce the ingredients to a fine paste in a liquidizer, add the eggs, nutmeg and seasoning and mix well. Check for taste.

Grease a set of timbale dishes or coffee cups with oil and fill them with the beetroot paste up to the rim. Cover tightly with pieces of greased aluminium foil and place in an oven dish, metal cake tin or cast-iron pan with a few centimetres of hot water in the bottom and cook in a 180°C oven for 20–30 mins. Check that the timbales are done by pricking with a toothpick, which should come out dry, or by pressing the top with your finger. When the timbale is firm to the touch it must be ready.

Prize the edges away from the side of each cup and tap it on a plate or working surface. Serve the timbale with fried ceps or other mushrooms and lingonberry sauce.

LINGONBERRY SAUCE:
1 tsp arrowroot or barley thickening
1.5 dl lingonberry juice
0.5 dl crème fraîche
50 g knobs of cold butter

Mix the arrowroot into a small quantity of the juice and beat into the remainder of the boiling juice. Add the crème fraîche and heat. Beat in the knobs of butter and check for taste.

TURNIP SOUP NINON FROM LIEKSA

3–4 small Finnish turnips, preferably grown in a clearing burned in the forest

1 medium-sized onion

a small piece of leek

a small piece of parsnip

100 g butter

7–8 dl thin meat or vegetable stock made from a stock cube

white pepper

grated nutmeg

1 bay leaf

a few sprigs of parsley

1 sprig of fresh thyme

2 dl cream

2 dl sparkling wine (preferably gooseberry and green currant wine in Finland)

2 dl whipped cream

Peel the vegetables and cut them into thumbnail-sized pieces. Melt the butter in a saucepan, add the onion and allow it to fry in the butter for a moment. Add the other vegetables and allow to simmer with the lid on for about 15 mins, stirring from time to time. Add the stock and the pepper and herbs in a small muslin bag or sieve so that they can easily be taken out before liquidizing.

Cook gently for 40 mins and then reduce to a velvety pulp in a liquidizer. Turn this pulp out into a saucepan and dilute with the cream. Season with salt and pepper as required.

Improve the soup by adding the sparkling wine and whipped cream. Stir and turn over gently with a ladle just before serving. This can be done at the table, while the guests are watching.

The custom of growing turnips in burned clearings began to die out at the same time as the potato was introduced into Finland and the clearing of patches of forest for cultivation purposes was prohibited. It is only from the 1980s onwards that people interested in our eating habits and tastes in food have developed a liking for turnips grown in this way.

Crème Ninon, a creamed pea soup enhanced with sparkling wine, is a classic of refined cuisine, but an equally distinguished flavour can be obtained using this Finnish variety of turnip.

AT LEAST TWICE A WEEK

At least that much fish anyone can eat, and many people far more, for all the talk of dioxins and other toxic substances. Finnish fish is healthy, nutritious and tasty. You should hear how the foreign visitors to our restaurant praise it!

The health experts say that you should ring the changes, eating a different species of fish each time, and that is in any case a good idea just so that you can appreciate the different flavours. Apart from the usual types of fish, this book has one recipe for roach and three for pike. It would be great if the Finns could learn to appreciate these fine fish again.

It can't be denied that we are a nation of fish-eaters. There are over 70,000 leisure-time fishermen registered with fishing clubs in this country, and over two million people go fishing at least once in the year. Fish that you have caught yourself is the ultimate in locally produced foodstuffs.

The next thing for anglers to learn is how to handle the fish after catching them. Gut them straight away and store them in the cold, and then put them straight into the pan while they are still fresh. And keep the backbone and head, as they make a wonderful base for a fish soup or sauce. Remember, too, that it's not always necessary to fillet a fish. It can make a simple, tasty meal just eaten "whole".

Insist on absolutely fresh fish when you buy it in a shop. Look for a fishmonger that you can trust, and ask where the fish was last swimming, when it died and what its journey to the shop was like. Our commercial fishermen have learned to handle their catches in a more professional way in recent years and are now able to fulfil their part of the delivery chain commendably. Now it is time to expect the same cold efficiency from the fishmongers.

COOK YOUR FISH LIGHTLY AND GENTLY, SO THAT IT STAYS JUICY AND TASTY. THE FINNS ARE ALL TOO PRONE TO FRY OR GRILL THEIR FISH UNTIL IT IS BLACK ON THE OUTSIDE AND DRY ALL THROUGH. A DELICATE REDNESS IN THE FLESH USUALLY SHOWS THAT THE FISH IS AT ITS TASTIEST.

THERE ARE SOME FISH PROCESSING FIRMS IN FINLAND WHO HAVE MANAGED TO DEVELOP THEIR PRODUCTS INTO HOUSEHOLD BYWORDS, PERHAPS THE BEST-KNOWN BEING THE PIIPANOJA COLD-SMOKED FISH AND SUNDOM SMOKED BALTIC HERRINGS. YOU CAN FIND THE PIIPANOJA SALMON AND BALTIC HERRINGS IN RESTAURANTS, MARKET HALLS AND SPECIALIZED DELICATESSENS AND THE SUNDOM BALTIC HERRINGS IN MORE GENERAL SHOPS AS WELL.

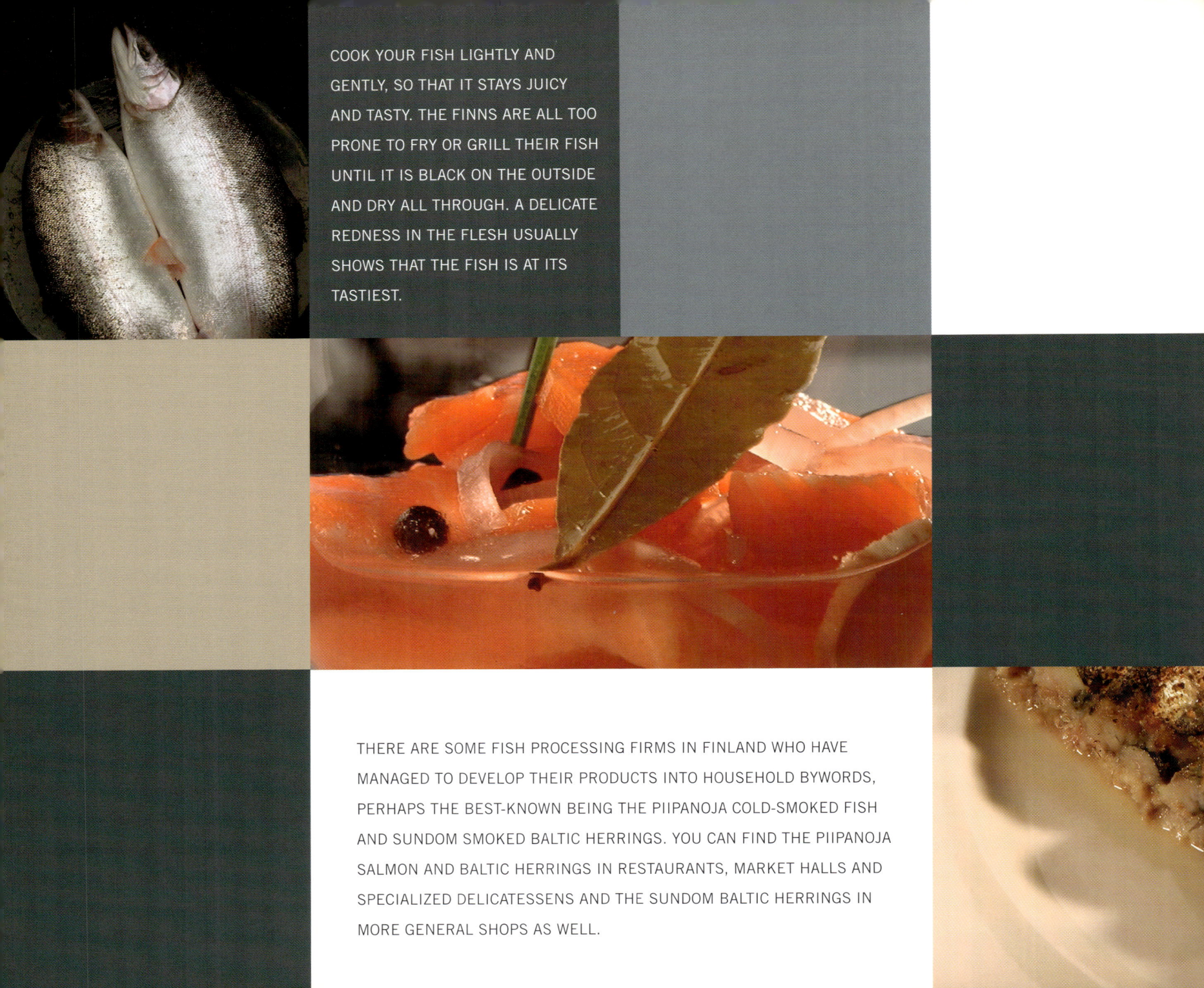

BOILED AND POACHED FISH IS REGAINING ITS DESERVED PLACE IN OUR DIET. IT COULD BE SERVED MORE GENERALLY IN RESTAURANTS, THOUGH. THE BEST ACCOMPANIMENTS FOR BOILED PIKE ARE A POT OF SHARP HORSERADISH AND A TRADITIONAL EGG SAUCE.

THE BALTIC HERRING IS ONE OF OUR FINEST FISHES AND A NATIONAL TREASURE, ALTHOUGH IT HAS UNFORTUNATELY BECOME SCARCE IN RECENT TIMES. THE BEST ONES, OF MEDIUM SIZE, COME NOWADAYS FROM THE QUARK AND OTHER PARTS OF THE GULF OF BOTHNIA. TO APPRECIATE THE FULL FLAVOUR, YOU SHOULD GUT AND FILLET THE HERRINGS YOURSELF, ALTHOUGH LESS WATER IS USED IN MACHINE FILLETING THAN WAS THE CASE EARLIER.

GLASSMASTER'S RAINBOW TROUT

a boneless fillet or other piece of rainbow trout

coarse salt

MARINADE:

5 dl water

2.5 dl sugar

2–3 carrots, cut into thin slices

1 onion, cut into rings

a piece of leek

10 allspice seeds, crushed

a few cloves

a bay leaf

Bring the water and sugar to the boil and then add the spices and vegetables.

PICKLING LIQUID:

1.5–2 dl spirit vinegar

2–3 pieces of horseradish

Add spirit vinegar to the marinade so that your cheeks tingle when you taste it. Cool it down and add the pieces of horseradish. They will keep the liquid clear.

Salt the fish lightly and allow it to stand for 2–3 hours. Cut it into finger-sized pieces and pour the cold marinade over these. Allow to marinade for a couple of days at least. Fish prepared in this way will keep in the fridge for quite a long time.

Serve with boiled potatoes.

ROACH TARTARE À LA JUHA NIEMIÖ

500 g lightly salted roach fillets
4 hard-boiled eggs, coarsely grated or chopped with a knife
1 finely chopped onion
1 dl finely chopped chives
3 tbsp chopped anchovies
1 tbsp strong mustard
1 tbsp mayonnaise

rapeseed oil
1 clove of garlic, roughly chopped
3–6 tomatoes
2–3 tbsp finely chopped capers

Skin the fish and cut it into small cubes or chop it quickly in a liquidizer. Add the other ingredients and shape into small cakes. Fry these quickly on both sides.

Heat the oil, add the garlic, the tomatoes cut in half and the capers. Heat again and place on the plate together with the roach tartare.

It is advisable to freeze the roach before use in order to eliminate any parasites.

Juha Niemiö is a respected member of the old guard of master chefs, who has been one of the leading figures in the Finnish international team of chefs and was executive chef at the Haikko Manor House for many years. He now occupies a similar position at the Bodega Salud restaurant in Tampere.

COLD-SMOKED BALTIC HERRING TARTARE WITH BEETROOT JELLY

250 g cold-smoked Baltic herring fillets
0.5 dl smetana
0.5 dl crème fraîche
1 tbsp slightly sweet mustard
a little lemon juice
black pepper from a mill
ground sea salt
1 shallot, finely chopped
a couple of sprigs of dill
2–3 leaves of chives

Skin the Baltic herring fillets and cut them into small cubes. Lightly whip the smetana and stir in the crème fraîche, mustard and seasoning. Finally add the Baltic herrings and shallot, making sure that the paste remains soft in texture. Finally add the finely chopped dill and chives. Serve out onto caraway-seed crispbread.

An excellent accompaniment is jellied beetroot.

JELLIED BEETROOT:
4 beetroots
1 tbsp butter
15–20 sugar lumps
0.5 dl red wine vinegar

Wash the beetroots and peel them well, as they have thick skins. Cut them first into slices and then into strips.

Melt the butter and brown the sugar lumps in it. Add all the vinegar at once and then the strips of beetroot. Cook gently for about half an hour, remembering to stir from time to time.

Finland is one of the world's principal producers of caraway seeds, and the oval, concave crispbread produced at the Åby Manor near Porvoo, which contains these seeds, is excellent for culinary purposes.

CRAYFISH SOUP WITH SKAGEN SALAD

10–15 small crayfish

1 carrot

a piece of parsnip

2 onions

a piece of fennel

1 clove of garlic

2–3 tbsp tomato purée

0.5 litre white wine

a dash of brandy

0.5 litre meat stock

1 sprig of thyme

2 bay leaves

3 sprigs of parsley

butter and flour for thickening

2 dl whipped cream

1 dl sparkling wine or champagne

Lightly fry the crayfish and dice the vegetables. They do not need to be peeled as long as they are washed thoroughly. Add the tomato purée and allow to simmer under a lid for a moment before adding the wine, brandy and meat stock.

Boil gently for an hour, then add the herbs and boil for a further 15 mins. Thicken with the butter and flour.

Add a couple of decilitres of loosely whipped cream and a dash of sparkling wine or champagne to the soup just before serving.

This delicious soup can also be made from frozen crab shells or shrimps with their shells intact.

Rinse and dry the shells left from a crayfish party, throwing away any remaining contents, including the legs. Dry the shells in a 120°C oven and freeze them for use later in this soup instead of whole crayfish.

SKAGEN SALAD:

100 g drained prawn tails (tinned or frozen)

2 dl chives, finely chopped

3–4 tbsp mayonnaise

1 tbsp tomato purée

a couple of drops of lemon juice

1 tbsp green currant wine

1 tbsp brandy

cayenne pepper

toasted bread

1–2 tsp fish roe

Roughly chop the prawns and mix them with the other ingredients. This prawn salad should be stiff but soft. Serve it out onto pieces of buttered toast and garnish with fish roe.

BAKED BALTIC HERRINGS WITH ANCHOVIES AND MASHED POTATO

1–2 onions, finely chopped

100 g butter for frying the onions

800 g Baltic herring fillets, preferably cleaned by hand

10 anchovy fillets

ground white pepper

salt

knobs of butter

water

a bunch of dill, finely chopped

Lightly fry the chopped onion in butter for about 5 mins and spread it on the bottom of an oven dish. Arrange the herring fillets in the dish, skin upwards and place an anchovy fillet inside every third one. Sprinkle white pepper and a little salt on them, but remember that the anchovy will also be quite salty.

Place the cold knobs of butter on the fillets and cover with water until about a third of the fillets are above the water. Bake in the oven at 180°C for 20 mins.

When the herrings are cooked, take the dish out of the oven and sprinkle the fish liberally with chopped dill.

Serve with mashed potato and a good slice of lemon.

FRIED OHTAKARI WHITEFISH WITH BEETROOT COOKED IN ORANGE JUICE

4 fillets of whitefish with the scales removed

salt

freshly ground white pepper

1 dl breadcrumbs

1 dl flour

butter for frying

Season the whitefish fillets with salt and pepper. Roll them in the mixture of flour and breadcrumbs and fry them in a hot pan until they are a golden brown.

BEETROOT COOKED IN ORANGE JUICE

3 beetroots

100 g butter

freshly ground white pepper

salt

grated nutmeg

3–4 dl freshly squeezed orange juice

Peel the beetroots and cut them into segments. Melt the butter in a saucepan, add the segments of beetroot and toss them in the butter for a minute or so. Season with salt, pepper and nutmeg. Add the orange juice, cover the saucepan with greaseproof paper and allow to simmer. This will boil off the excess liquid, and the beetroots will be cooked in 20–25 mins.

Take the beetroots out and boil the juice to concentrate it a little. Return the beetroots to the juice and serve with the freshly fried whitefish.

Boiled potatoes are a suitable accompaniment for this dish. If there is a shortage of space on the stove, brown the fish in the frying pan and then cook it in the oven for a few minutes just before serving.

The island of Ohtakari off the coast of Lohtaja has been famous for its fishing village and whitefish catches since the 16th century.

IN MARKUS' OPINION

A NEW PREDICAMENT FOR FISHERMEN

Fishing restrictions, seals, irrational price competition and many other problems have led large numbers of fishermen to give up their time-honoured profession.

The coastal town of Hanko, for instance, apparently has only one full-time fisherman working all the year round, and Helsinki has only one Finnish herring trawler left. The only large, ultra-modern trawler working in the Gulf of Bothnia was recently sold to Ireland because the fishing restrictions made it unprofitable to operate in Finnish waters.

One friend who is a fisherman tells me that the average age of the men employed in his profession is well over 50 years. How many sons of fishermen would be prepared to go fishing under the ice in winter without even getting a decent wage for their work?

As one of my own suppliers, *Esa Lahtinen,* manager of a fish processing firm in Uusikaupunki, is constantly reminding me, fish farming is becoming more important than ever in Finland. Without it there would soon be no Finnish fish in the shops at all. Then we would be relying on imported fish and prices would be astronomical.

People still tend to scorn rainbow trout and other farmed fish without any good reason, mostly on account of prejudices that go back for decades, to times when they were of rather doubtful quality. Nowadays rainbow trout are usually fairly consistent in quality and size and extremely tasty. Esa also claims that complaints about the ecological drawbacks of fish farming are outdated.

Now fish farms in Finland have started raising whitefish as well. This fine species has been difficult to come by for a long time, and the farmed variety has firm flesh and is easy to handle. Unofficial blind testing has shown that even professional caterers are unable to tell the difference between farmed and "wild" whitefish.

So the situation is by no means hopeless. The fish processing company owned by Esa Lahtinen and Pekka Vapanen has about a dozen contracted suppliers and about 250 associated fishermen who are committed to certain quality criteria and standards for the handling of catches. The fish reach the processing plant within a few hours and are frozen or vacuum-packed in an absolutely fresh condition.

Eat plenty of fish! At least twice a week.

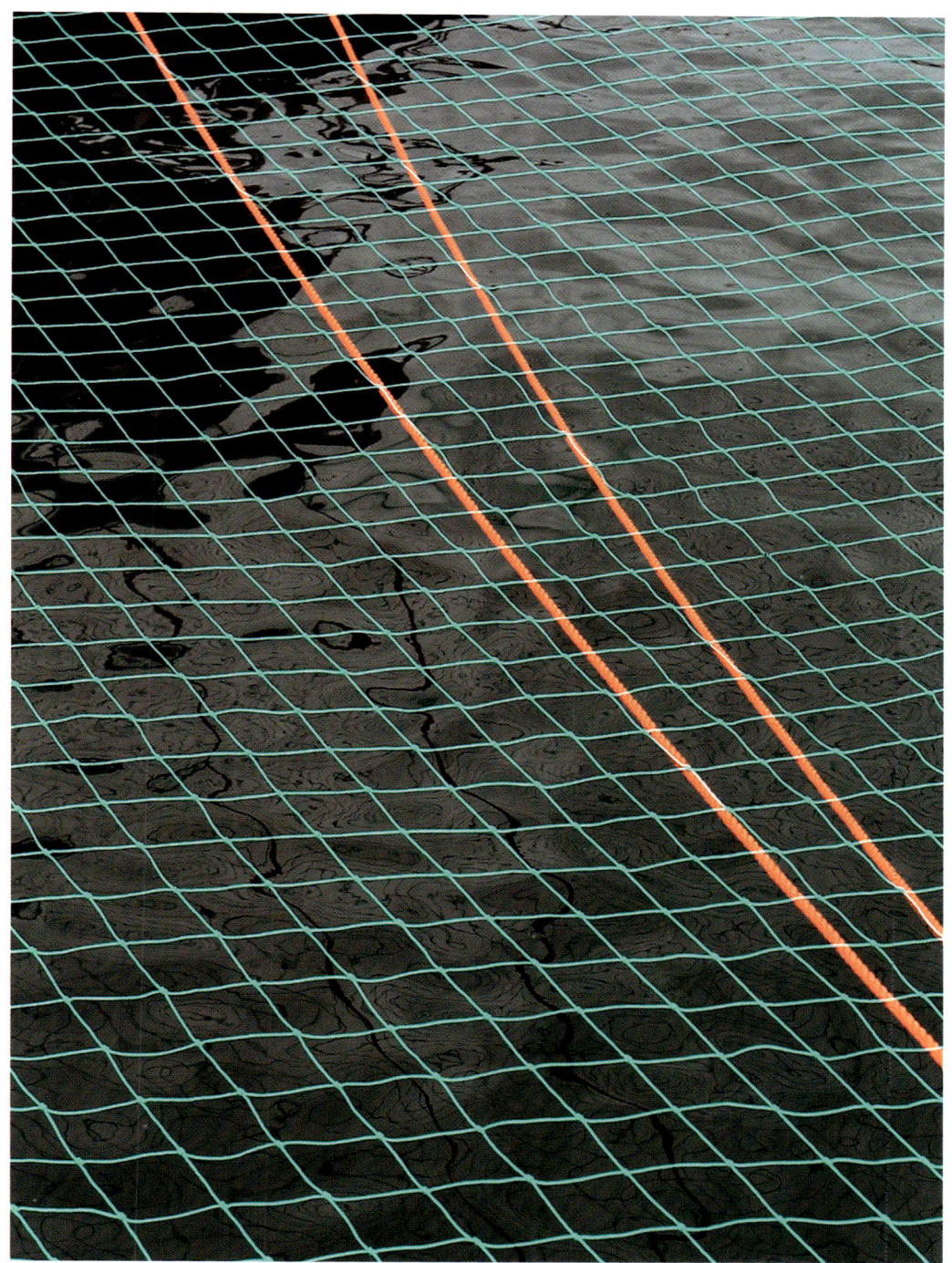

CHARR SHASHLIK WITH CHANTERELLES

pieces of fresh onion
650–850 g good quality rainbow trout
rapeseed oil

Blanch the onion quickly and cool it in cold water. Skin the rainbow trout and cut it crossways into thick slices. Thread the pieces of fish and onion on barbeque skewers and brush their surfaces with oil.

Heat a cast-iron frying pan on the stove until it is very hot and grill the shashlik sticks on all sides. Then cook them in a 170°C oven for 5–8 mins.

Serve with sautéed chanterelles and new potatoes.

SAUTÉED CHANTERELLES
500 g chanterelles
butter for frying
4 tbsp wine vinegar
0.5 dl water
80–100 g butter
black pepper from a mill
1 dl finely chopped green onion stems

Sauté the chanterelles in butter in a frying pan.

Heat a saucepan well and pour in the vinegar. Add the water and bring to the boil. Stir in the knobs of butter and return to the boil. Finally add the black pepper, onion stems and fried chanterelles.

The rainbow trout farmed in Finland originally came from Canada and is a close relative of the Arctic charr. It was apparently President Kekkonen who first likened it to salmon, and the name has stuck. In the early days it varied greatly in quality, from rather dubious to tolerable, but nowadays Finnish farmed rainbow trout is an excellent fish, and it is for this reason that we have begun to refer to it as charr in our restaurant.

SALMON AND POTATO CASSEROLE À LA MARKUS

1 kg semi-floury potatoes, peeled

about 500 g Baltic Sea salmon or good quality rainbow trout, skinned, boned and filleted

3–4 eggs

3 dl whipping cream

2 dl milk

nutmeg

ground allspice

ground white pepper from a mill

1 tsp salt

100–200 g butter for greasing the dish and glazing the casserole

a bunch of dill, finely chopped

Cut the potatoes into slices two or three millimetres thick with a food processor or by hand. Rinse them quickly under cold water, drain in a sieve and dry on a cloth or with kitchen paper. Cut the fish into 0.5–1 cm slices.

Break the eggs and stir them carefully into the cream and milk. Mix in the spices and salt.

Grease an oven dish, line the bottom with a 1–2 cm layer of potato and cover this evenly with the slices of fish. Top with another 1 cm layer of potato and pour the egg and milk mixture onto this so that it is practically covered.

Bake in a 220°C oven for about ten minutes. Smooth the top surface of the potato with a spatula and add knobs of butter. Reduce the oven temperature to 175°C and bake for a further 50–60 mins. If the surface begins to brown too quickly cover it with aluminium foil or damp greaseproof paper.

Test whether the casserole is cooked sufficiently by picking it with a cocktail stick or knife. If this goes through the layers easily it is done. Take the dish out of the oven and cover it with foil. Allow to stand for 15–30 mins to even out the temperature, then serve out suitable portions onto plates with fresh cucumber salad or pickled beetroot.

A good sauce for this is melted butter with plenty of finely chopped dill in it.

It is good to salt the fish lightly a couple of hours beforehand, so that the casserole will be more evenly salted.

Semi-floury potatoes are best for this salmon casserole, as very floury ones will absorb too much of the moisture and disintegrate, while very firm ones will remain too hard.

YOUNG PIKE LACED WITH ANCHOVY IN A DILL AND CREAM SAUCE

600–800 g young pike fillets

salt

freshly ground white pepper

8 anchovy fillets

butter for frying

2 dl whipping cream

0.5 dl white currant wine or dry white wine

a bunch of dill, finely chopped

Skin the pike fillets and cut them into pieces about ten centimetres long. Season with salt and pepper. Make a cut about 1/2–1 cm deep in the back of each and insert a piece of anchovy fillet.

Brown the pieces of pike on both sides in butter, arrange them in a suitably sized dish and pour the cream and wine over them so that they are more than half covered.

Cook in the oven at 180°C for about ten minutes. Then take the pieces of fish out and pour the liquid into a saucepan and add the dill. Reduce the liquid on a high heat for a couple of minutes so that the sauce thickens.

The bones and head of the pike, without the gills, can be used with very little effort to make an excellent stock as the basis for a fish soup.

PIKE QUENELLES WITH NETTLE SAUCE

about 400 g skinless pike fillets
1–2 tsp salt
white pepper from a mill
grated rind of half a lemon
a little grated nutmeg
1 large egg (or 2 small ones)
2.5 dl whipping cream
0.5 dl smetana
(1 tsp brandy)
butter for greasing the dish
0.5 dl dry white wine or green currant wine

Cut the pike fillets into finger-sized strips, season with salt, pepper and grated lemon rind and nutmeg. Put the mixture on one side for half an hour to even out the flavour and give it the right texture.

Separate the white and yolk of the egg. Grind the fish to an even paste in a liquidizer or multipurpose mixer, add the egg white, and when a firm mixture has been obtained add the yolk as well. Then pour the whipping cream in gently, stirring all the time. When the cream has been absorbed completely and the paste is sufficiently firm, carefully stir in the smetana. Finally add a teaspoonful of brandy to crown the quenelle mixture.

Make a small trial pat of the mixture to fry or boil. If you are satisfied with it, form the whole of the paste into egg-sized balls or nuggets with two spoons and placed them in an oven dish greased with butter. Sprinkle the wine on the bottom of the dish and cover with aluminium foil tucked tightly around the edges of the dish.

Cook in a 170°C oven for about 20 mins or until the quenelles are done, or instead you can cook them for a few minutes in gently boiling salt water.

All the ingredients should be taken straight from the fridge so as to be suitably cold at the beginning.

NETTLE SAUCE:

about 2 litres of young nettle leaves or tops, or the equivalent amount of fresh spinach
a knob of butter
half an onion, finely chopped
1 tsp flour
3 dl cream
(a little milk)

Put the nettles into boiling salt water and return to the boil. Tip them into a sieve and rinse in cold running water to stop them cooking and prevent them from turning dark in colour. Squeeze the nettle leaves as dry as possible and chop them with a knife. Melt the butter in a saucepan and add the chopped onion. Lightly fry this for a moment and then add the nettles. Fry for a few minutes, then sprinkle flour on them and mix it in carefully. Add the cream and allow to simmer for 5–10 mins. If the sauce becomes too thick add a little milk.

Serve with rice or boiled pearl barley. Boiled potatoes also go well with this dish.

PIKE POACHED IN COOLING STOCK, WITH BROWNED HORSERADISH BUTTER

a whole pike weighing less than 1.5 kg, scaled and gutted, without gills

coarse salt

100 g butter

about 2 tbsp grated horseradish

1–2 hard-boiled eggs

parsley

STOCK:

1 carrot, in small pieces

1 onion in segments

2 bay leaves

8–10 white peppers

8–10 seeds of allspice

2 litres water

Salt the pike a couple of hours before cooking. Put all the other ingredients for the stock into the cold water, bring them to the boil and simmer for about twenty minutes to release the flavour from the vegetables and seasoning.

If the fish is too big to go into the saucepan whole, cut it into steaks a couple of centimetres thick. Put the fish into the stock so that it is completely immersed. Bring almost to the boil and then take the saucepan off the heat and allow the fish to cook in the stock for about 20–30 mins as it cools down.

Heat the butter in a frying pan until it is nut-brown and add the grated horseradish just before serving. The grated horseradish can also be served separately.

A traditional way of serving the browned melted butter would be to add chopped hard-boiled egg with a little finely chopped parsley in it.

Well boiled, firm-textured potatoes are a good accompaniment to this dish.

Poaching in a cooling stock is not only a straightforward way of cooking any fish but also a surprisingly delicate way of doing it, allowing the aromas of the fish itself to be savoured at their best. The younger the pike the better!

THE REVIVAL OF FLAVOURSOME PORK

If a pig could decide itself where it was to live it would probably choose the Heikkola piggery in Iitti and become one of Benjamin's Well-Kept Porkers. It would have clean, comfortable wood shavings to lie on and plenty of space to root about and gambol, and it would be fed on barley and oats from its own master's fields or the neighbouring ones, with a dessert of fine hay.

And if I could choose what pork I use in my cooking, I would go for just such a piggery. The problem in Finland is that we have been trying for so long to achieve such large production volumes and such low fat percentages in our pork that it no longer has any taste.

Ismo and *Eila Eerola,* who run the piggery and the farm sales outlet put less emphasis on growth rates and production costs and prefer to concentrate on taste and quality. The breeding side of the business is looked after by a partner living the same district, and the slaughterhouse is almost as close. The market is so well organized that the whole carcass is sold fresh within a week.

The Eerolas put their trust in flavoursome, tender pork, and it is to be hoped that many more piggeries run on the same principle will be opened in Finland. Even now the Heikkola farm is by no means the only one.

It is said that a pig that is satisfied with life has a tightly curled tail. This seems to be the fashion for tails at Heikkola.

THE BEST PORK IN FINLAND COMES FROM PIGS THAT ARE CROSSES BETWEEN THREE OR FOUR PARTICULAR BREEDS AND HAVE BEEN FED ON 80% LOCALLY GROWN CEREALS.

A MODERN PIGGERY IS ENVIRONMENTALLY FRIENDLY. THE FLOOR COVERING OF WOOD SHAVINGS PREVENTS THE MANURE FROM ESCAPING AND YIELDS A COMPOST THAT CAN BE SPREAD ON THE FIELDS, NATURE'S OWN RECYCLING METHOD.

TWO-THIRDS OF THE FAT IN PORK IS SOFT AND HEALTHY TO EAT. IT IS THE FAT THAT GIVES THE MEAT ITS FLAVOUR, BUT YOU DON'T NEED TO EAT THE VISIBLE FAT LAYER.

GOURMETS HAVE LEARNED TO APPRECIATE THE CHEAPER CUTS OF MEAT AS WELL: THE NECK, BELLY AND LEG, FOR EXAMPLE. YOU CAN STILL BUY OX-TAIL FROM GOOD MEAT COUNTERS AND SPECIALIZED BUTCHERS' SHOPS, AT LEAST IF YOU ORDER IT IN ADVANCE.

ORGANICALLY RAISED MINCED MEAT STEAK WITH SAUNA-CURED HAM

0.5 dl soft white breadcrumbs
1 dl cream
1/2 onion
butter for frying
200 g sauna-cured ham
400 g minced organically raised pork
1 egg
ground allspice
2 tbsp Åland mustard
1–2 tsp salt

Put the breadcrumbs into the cream to soak. Finely chop the onion, lightly fry it in butter and allow to cool. Mince the ham, breadcrumbs and onion together to a finely ground mixture in a mill or liquidizer, and then carefully combine all the ingredients to form an even paste and place it in the fridge to stand for a while. It will then be easier to work with.

Shape the mixture into suitable-sized steaks or bars, brown them in butter and then cook them in a 180°C oven for a couple of minutes.

Serve with creamed carrot.

CREAMED CARROT:
3 carrots, peeled
1/2 onion
2–3 tbsp butter
2 tbsp flour
4 dl full-cream milk
grated nutmeg
white pepper from a mill
salt

Slice the carrots and finely chop the onion. Melt the butter and add the onion. Cook for a moment and then add the slices of carrot. Cook the mixture for a couple of minutes, stirring it a few times. Add the flour and stir carefully.

Pour in the milk in small doses, stirring constantly. Allow the mixture to simmer for about 15 mins or until the carrots are cooked but still firm. Season with nutmeg, white pepper and salt.

Serve with the steaks, and with a few boiled potatoes if desired.

BELLY OF PORK STUFFED WITH FRUIT

a 1–1.5 kg piece of organically raised or otherwise good quality rib of pork, boneless but with the skin intact

half a handful of sea salt

100 g dried apricots

100 g dried figs

2 tbsp potato flour

Rub salt into the skin of the pork and allow to stand for a day or so. Soak the dried apricots and figs in plenty of water for the same length of time, then drain them and dry them well. Sprinkle them with potato flour to absorb their juice. Mix well.

Cut a pocket lengthways in the joint of pork leaving the two parts attached at the sides. Fill the pocket entirely with the fruit.

Place the meat on an oven tray, skin upwards and set the temperature at 130°C for the first hour. Reduce the temperature to 100°C and roast the joint for a further three hours, still with the skin side upwards. Then turn it over and cook for another 2–3 hours at the same temperature. Finally turn the oven out and open the door slightly, leaving the meat to stand in the oven for another hour or so, covered with aluminium foil.

Cut the meat into slices about a centimetre thick. This can also be done when the meat is cold, heating it gently once more before serving.

This dish is best served with steamed red cabbage and a mashed potato made of floury potatoes, cream and butter. A dish of mashed swede baked in the oven, as typically served at Christmas in Finland, also goes well with this meat. The liquid from the roasting of the meat will make a good sauce.

A tender piece of belly of pork is also a useful alternative to ham at Christmas and makes an excellent meal at other times of year.

CARELIAN STEW À LA MARKUS

This recipe should include about 1 dl of chopped vegetables (or 4–6 good-sized pieces) per person. There should be three or four sorts of meat, about 180 g of each, cut into largish lumps.

shoulder of veal
shoulder of young reindeer
shoulder of pork
shoulder of lamb

whole shallots

whole carrots, peeled

turnips, peeled and cut into segments

butter for browning

4–8 bay leaves

8–10 seeds of allspice, ground

1 tbsp ground black pepper

salt

a couple of sprigs each of parsley, thyme and rosemary

water

Rinse the meat in cold water and dry it on a cloth. Brown it and the vegetables on all sides in butter and arrange all the ingredients, seasoning and herbs in layers in a cooking pot. Pour water on them until they are two-thirds covered. Put the lid on and cook in a 220°C oven for half an hour.

Lower the temperature to 110°C and allow to simmer for three to four hours or until the meat is tender. Take out the meat and vegetables and put them in a serving dish, then reduce the liquid by boiling hard. Sieve the liquid, check for taste and serve as a sauce with the meat.

Boiled potatoes and grated fresh root vegetables go well with this dish.

You can choose the meat for Carelian stew quite freely according to what you fancy and what is on offer. It was the custom in Carelia to add offal or game sometimes. The local shallots supplied to me by Matti Veijola, which have been judged superior in flavour to either Central European or Mediterranean onions, crown this dish perfectly, but you can also use yellow onions if you wish.

OX-TAIL AND BARLEY RISOTTO

1/2 root celeriac

2 onions

2 parsnips

8–12 pieces of ox-tail (1–1.5 kg)

butter and rapeseed oil for browning

coarse sea salt

about 10 black peppers

4–6 sprigs of thyme or rosemary

4 bay leaves

a couple of strips of lemon peel

water

Cut all the vegetables into thumbnail-sized pieces. Brown the pieces of ox-tail on all sides in the mixture of butter and rapeseed oil and season with salt and pepper. Brown the vegetables in the same pan and place them in the bottom of an oven dish, with the pieces of ox-tail on top.

Add the herbs and other seasoning. Pour a couple of decilitres of water into the frying pan and bring to the boil. Scrape the bottom of the pan with a spatula and pour the liquid through a sieve onto the ox-tail pieces in the oven dish. Add more water if necessary so that the meat is about a third covered by the liquid. Cook in a 120°C oven for three to four hours.

When the ox-tail pieces are cooked, take them out of the dish and strain the liquid into a saucepan. Reduce a little by boiling so that about 1.5 dl remains. Whisk a few knobs of butter into the sauce and bring to the boil.

Serve the ox-tail with barley risotto or mashed potatoes.

BARLEY RISOTTO:

2 dl barley grains

1 carrot

1/2 onion

butter for frying

water or meat stock

1 tsp salt

Soak the barley grains in water overnight, sieve and drain as dry as possible.

Chop the carrot and onion into small pieces, fry them lightly in the butter for a few moments and then add the barley. Stir them together a few times and then add water or meat stock to cover the risotto generously. Season with salt, put the lid on and simmer for about 40 mins or until the barley is cooked.

Barley is a Finnish alternative to rice. Its cooking time can be shortened by soaking it in water first.

MARKUS THE CHEF'S PORK SAUSAGE SOUP

**300–400 g firm potatoes,
e.g. Bintje, Victoria or Asterix**

1 carrot

a piece of celeriac

a piece of parsnip

1 onion

the white part of a leek

100 g butter for frying

about 1.5 litres thin meat stock

300 g "siskonmakkara" pork sausages

2–3 bay leaves

8–10 seeds of allspice, ground

5–6 black peppers, ground

parsley

Peel and dice the potatoes and cut the other root vegetables into slightly smaller cubes. Finely chop the onion and leek and fry them lightly in butter first. Then add the potatoes and other vegetables. Put the pan on one side with its lid on for about ten minutes for the vegetables to soften gradually.

In the meantime bring the meat stock to the boil. This should preferably be of your own making, but a stock cube will do. Squeeze small balls of the sausage meat out of the skins by hand and drop them into the bubbling stock, cook them gently for a couple of minutes and then take them out of the stock to wait.

Pour the stock over the vegetables and cook them gently together with the seasoning until they are soft, then add the balls of sausage meat. Add plenty of finely chopped parsley to the soup just before serving.

Siskonmakkara is a small, light-coloured traditional Finnish pork sausage intended to be cooked by boiling. My favourite ones are those made by Veijo Wotkin, the best-known connoisseur and supplier of meats for the restaurants in Helsinki, whose products are also on sale at his own factory outlet and in many of the best grocery stores.

FINNISH SHEEP ARE THE REAL THING!

The lambs born on the Bovik organic sheep farm in spring are ready to go out to graze in the fields and on the islands and shore meadows by the summer. Under the EU support agreement they are responsible for managing the traditional biotopes and promoting biodiversity in the cultural landscapes of the area throughout the summer months, taking their food from these natural pastures. When autumn comes they return to dozens of small patches of field in Snappertuna and Karjalohja to gourmandize on grass and clover, after which it is back to the sheep pen and winter feed.

The farm takes good care of its livestock, and this is also reflected in the taste of the meat. The young organic lamb from Bovik won the first prize for the best culinary raw material in the Finnish Gastronomy Fair in spring 2004, and the delicious sausages produced from the same meat by this farm in collaboration with some local firms also enjoy a high reputation, not to mention the soft knitted garments made by *Ülle Nurmi* from pure, undyed lamb's wool.

The sheep at Bovik are of the traditional Finnish breed, for which a breeders' association now exists to promote its production and quality. It is worth preserving the Finnish breed of sheep if only for the wonderful flavour of its meat, claims *Sebastian Nurmi,* manager of the Bovik farm and the photographer responsible for the illustrations in this book.

The sheep of the Åland Islands are similarly renowned for their delicious meat, the majority of which ends up in the hands of one butcher with stalls in the Old Market Hall and Hakaniemi Market Hall in Helsinki. "We buy some 3500 kg of lamb from Åland each year and every bit of it is sold, either on our stalls or direct to restaurants," the butcher *Kjell Söderlund* explains. High quality lamb is also produced nowadays around the northern tip of the Gulf of Bothnia, and eastern Finland is a traditional lamb-rearing area.

Even so, people in Finland don't eat very much lamb, and at present there are only about 80,000 ewes in the whole country, most of them of the traditional Finnish breed.

All credit is due to the meat suppliers for the work they have done to produce really high quality Finnish lamb. Now what we need is more sheep farms and more Finnish lamb in the shops!

IN MARKUS' OPINION

I use a lot of Finnish lamb in my cooking, and I have my own supplier whom I can rely on to send me the very best meat.

"When you buy Finnish lamb it really is lamb and not mutton in disguise," my friend *Kjell Söderlund* emphasizes. And that makes a big difference.

The greatest demand for lamb in this country is at Easter, although the meat is at its most delicious in the autumn, which is the natural slaughtering time. Many sheep farmers nowadays try to slaughter some of their animals at Easter, however, and frozen meat from the autumn will retain its flavour pretty well.

Lamb would make a fine meal for Christmas as well, come to that!

Roast lamb calls for great care with the cooking time, as it is at its best when the meat still has a beautiful rosy tinge inside. With lamb cutlets it's quite enough just to show them the hot pan.

The cheaper cuts of lamb have become fashionable in recent times. The leg and neck and cuts intended for soup or for stewing need to be cooked slowly, but when well done you can almost eat them with a spoon.

Minced lamb straight from the grinder is marvellous for everyday use at home. Meat balls of lamb are a great delicacy in many parts of the world, although the mutton used for them is not a patch on our real lamb.

The old Finnish method of cooking lamb in a fire pit in the ground is not easy to do well, but there are some people who specialize in it, and when successful the result can be a true experience.

SHOULDER OF LAMB COOKED IN FOIL

1 shoulder of young lamb on the bone
coarse sea salt
8–16 whole cloves of garlic
8–12 whole small onions
6–8 largish pieces of carrot
4–6 pieces of celery or
cubes of celeriac
a bunch of fresh thyme
a few sprigs of fresh rosemary
ground black pepper
1–2 dl water
a generous knob of butter

a large sheet of aluminium foil
1 dl rapeseed oil

Rub the coarse salt into the shoulder of lamb and place it on the greased foil together with the vegetables and seasoning. Sprinkle with water and a generous knob of butter and fold into a tight package.

Put the package in a 220°C oven for 20 mins and then reduce the temperature to 110°. Cook for another three hours. Open the package and serve.

A good accompaniment is garlic mayonnaise.

SLOWLY COOKED SHANK OF LAMB WITH CHERRY TOMATO AND ONION SALAD

4 shanks of lamb
5–6 sprigs of thyme
5–6 sprigs of rosemary
a few cloves of garlic, crushed
1 tbsp ground black pepper
coarse salt
butter and rapeseed oil for browning
about 1 litre meat stock or water
3 dl white currant wine or dry white wine
4 whole shallots
2–3 bay leaves

Season the shanks of lamb with the herbs and garlic, rub pepper, salt and garlic into their surfaces and allow them to stand for about 24 hours. Then brown them on all sides in a mixture of butter and oil.

Place them in an oven dish and add enough of the meat stock or water and wine to half cover them. More liquid will be needed if the dish is a wide one. Place the herbs, shallots and bay leaves on top, cover with a lid and allow to cook overnight in an 80°C oven.

Serve with cherry tomato and onion salad. Thicken the juice from the meat to use as a gravy.

CHERRY TOMATO AND ONION SALAD:

10–14 cherry tomatoes
the white part of a leek
butter for frying
salt
pepper
juice from the cooking of the lamb

Make a small cut in the top of each of the tomatoes and drop them into boiling water for a couple of seconds. This will soften the skin so that it can be pulled off. Then dip the tomatoes in cold water to prevent them from cooking.

Cut the leek into thin rings and lightly fry them in a small amount of butter. Add the tomatoes and stir them round in the pan for a moment so that they warm up. Season with salt and pepper. Finally add a little of the juice in which the meat was cooked.

LAMB AND CABBAGE ROLLS

1 medium-sized cabbage

1 onion

a knob of butter for frying

300 g minced lamb

100 g ready-cooked barley or rice porridge

1 egg

salt

white pepper from a mill

four-spice condiment

1 dl syrup

100 g melted butter

2 dl cream

Remove the stump of the cabbage by making a conical-shaped incision in the bottom. Put it in salt water to boil with the lid on and strip off the outside leaves as they soften. An alternative would be to remove the outside leaves raw and then boil the rest of the cabbage until soft.

Cut out the thickest of the leaf stems. Lightly fry the onion in butter and then combine the minced meat, porridge and chopped onion. Add the egg. Season with salt, white pepper and four-spice condiment. Divide out the mixture onto the cabbage leaves and roll them into suitable-sized packages.

Place the rolls on a greased oven tray and brush with a mixture of syrup and melted butter. Cook in a 220° oven for 15 mins and then reduce the temperature to 160°. Cook for a further hour, basting them with the syrup mixture from time to time. Add the cream about halfway through.

After taking the rolls out of the oven, sieve the liquid into a saucepan and thicken. Serve with crushed lingonberries and mashed potato.

DELICIOUS POULTRY!

It's a fine thing that at last you can find high quality farmed poultry in Finland: grain-fed chickens, turkeys, geese and both wild and domestic ducks.

On one journey north from Helsinki to Lapland we stopped near Mikkeli at the Hauhala Farm at Anttola, where *Virpi* and *Antti Rantalainen,* on taking the farm over, chose to specialize in raising geese. Their main customers are restaurants, but their products have also begun to appear in the shops recently.

There were about 4000 squawking white geese strutting about between the sprinklers in the fields, enjoying the summer sun. At that stage they were feeding only on grass, but when young, and also after the outdoor grazing season comes to an end, they receive a nutritious artificial feed. They are never force-fed, however: it all depends on their own appetite, which means that you can savour Hauhala's goose liver pâté with a clear conscience.

Hauhala also has Finland's only slaughterhouse and butchery that specializes entirely in geese, producing not only fresh meat but also pâté and delicately smoked, slightly salted fillets for the cold meat counters of delicatessens.

Another of my poultry favourites is duck from the Alhopakka Farm, of a quality guaranteed by the expertise of *Markku Pietilä.*

Duck and goose fat, by the way, is some of the best you can get for frying and can be used with both poultry and delicacies of other kinds.

TRADITIONAL WILD DUCK CASSEROLE

2 wild ducks

0.5 litre root vegetables for stock: carrot, parsnip, celeriac and onion

juice of 1 lemon

salt

black pepper from a mill

3 bay leaves

1 sprig each of rosemary, thyme and parsley

1–2 litres water or meat stock made from powder or a cube (or diluted stock concentrate)

Clean the ducks and bind them, or at least their wings, with cotton thread. Dice the root vegetables. Brown the ducks carefully in their own fat in a frying pan by allowing the fat to melt from under their skin. Rub them with lemon, salt and pepper. Brown their necks and wings and also the diced vegetables.

Spread the vegetables and herbs in an even layer on the bottom of a casserole and place the ducks on top. Heat the liquid and pour it in so that the birds are about half covered. Cook in an oven at 180°C for about an hour. Begin with the birds placed breast upwards and turn them over about halfway through the cooking time. Allow them to cool in the stock and cut the breast and leg meat away from the bone. Leave the wing meat on the bone.

Put the bones back into the stock and allow to simmer on a gentle heat for as long as possible, but no more than six hours, adding more water if the liquid begins to boil dry. Strain the stock and use it to make the sauce, see below.

Serve the duck meat with game and cream sauce, green salad, red cabbage and fried potatoes.

GAME AND CREAM SAUCE:

35 g butter

30 g flour

4 dl reduced liquid from cooking of the ducks, or stock concentrate

0.5 dl lingonberries or cranberries

blackcurrant jelly or preserve

about 1 tbsp blue cheese

2 dl cream

a dash of brandy

Melt the butter, add the flour and stir well.

Add the berries to the strained stock to provide a little acidity. Cook gently for a couple of minutes. Thicken by whisking the mixture of butter and flour into the stock. Add the jelly, cheese and cream. Cook for another five minutes or so and strain. Spice with a dash of brandy.

BOILED RED CABBAGE:

1 kg red cabbage

100 g pork fat or butter

2 dl red wine vinegar

cloves

a piece of ginger, fresh or dried

a piece of cinnamon pod

1 bay leaf

about 10 whole black peppers

salt

a small piece of smoked belly of pork

2 dl syrup

Cut the red cabbage into thin strips. Melt the fat in a saucepan and add the cabbage. Allow to soften in the fat for a moment and then add the vinegar, the herbs wrapped in muslin and the piece of smoked belly of pork.
Allow to simmer for about two hours on a low heat, stirring from time to time. Add the syrup towards the end of the cooking time.

BREAST OF DUCK WITH RHUBARB SAUCE

4 breasts of duck
salt
white pepper from a mill
1 onion, cut into half-rings
4 tsp grated fresh ginger
3 dl rhubarb, cut into 1 cm cubes
4 tbsp honey
3 sprigs of parsley, chopped
2 dl green currant wine

Cut slits into the skin of the duck breasts, but not down to the flesh, rub with salt and pepper and allow the seasoning to sink in for a moment.

Put the breasts in a frying pan, skin side down, and then turn the heat on under them, so that the meat warms up slowly, some of the fat melts and the skin becomes crisp. Pour off the excess fat from time to time.

When the skin side is sufficiently crisp, turn the meat over and brown on the other side. Then take the meat out of the pan, wrap it in foil to retain the juice and allow it to stand for a while.

Put the onion rings in the same hot pan and lightly fry for a moment. Add the ginger and immediately afterwards the rhubarb, honey and parsley. Pour the wine over these ingredients and allow them to simmer for ten minutes.

Cut the duck breasts into slices and serve with boiled rice and the rhubarb compôte.

The domestic ducks that I use are supplied by Markku Pietilä of Pornainen, who raises them for 53 days on a diet of dried peas and his own blend of grains.

Breast of duck goes best with cherries, raspberries or currants – berries that are suitably sweet and sharp at the same time.

ST. MARTIN'S DAY ROAST GOOSE

1 whole goose
salt
white pepper
3 apples, cut into segments
1 dl plums or prunes
0.5 dl dried apricots
juice of 1 lemon
2 tbsp honey

Clean the inside of the goose and rub salt and pepper into it. Fill the stomach cavity with the fruit and tie the opening up with cotton thread. Rub lemon juice, salt and pepper into the surface of the goose.

Warm the honey a little and brush the surface of the goose with it. Place the goose on an oven grid, with a tray underneath to catch the dripping fat.

Roast for about 15 mins in a 230°C oven, lower the temperature to 180° and roast for about another 40 mins, and then lower the temperature again to 140° and roast for another hour or so. To make sure that the surface is crisp, brush it from time to time with the fat that has dropped onto the tray.

When cooked, take the goose out of the oven and allow to cool for a moment. You can either cut the meat ready or else carve the goose at the table.

Serve with roast potatoes and the fruit used to stuff the goose. For a sauce, use the game and cream sauce (p. 97) with some of the fat and stock from the goose whipped in and spiced with a spoonful of vodka just before serving.

It is common to serve black soup (recipe on the next page) with the St. Martin's Day goose.

BLACK SOUP

a piece of cinnamon pod, a piece of ginger, a few crushed white peppers, a few crushed black peppers and a couple of cloves

1.5 dl stock from the goose, or meat stock

6 dl goose or pig's blood

1 tbsp flour

2–3 tbsp red wine vinegar

port wine

madeira

2–3 tbsp syrup

cognac

Cook the spices gently in the goose or meat stock for about half an hour without letting the stock bubble. Strain the stock and combine it with the blood. Add the flour and vinegar and stir well.

Put the soup in the top part of a double cooker and steam for about 20 mins, stirring all the time, until cooked. The result should be a soft, velvety soup with a shiny surface. Check the sweetness and adjust with the port wine, madeira and syrup. Add a dash of cognac to sharpen the taste.

The traditional accompaniment served with the soup is a sausage made from the neck skin of the goose stuffed with a mixture of nearly cooked rice porridge, goose liver, raisins and egg, and often with the gizzard and heart of the goose as well.

The offal would be chopped finely and mixed into the porridge together with the egg, and this mixture would then be squeezed into the neck skin and sewn up. The sausages would then be cooked gently in boiling salt water or goose stock. Sometimes the wings of the goose would be served separately with the soup, alongside the sausage.

The soup should be heated, with constant stirring, just before serving. It should not be boiled fast, however, as this will cause it to go runny.

TURKEY SHASHLIK WITH WARM FRUIT COMPÔTE

500 g filleted turkey breasts

butter or rapeseed oil for browning

4–6 stems of young onions or chopped leeks

250 g fresh plums

250 g strawberries

3 dl semi-sweet strawberry wine

Cut the turkey fillets into suitable-sized pieces and thread them onto four shashlik skewers. Brown in butter or oil and then place them in an oven dish and cook for 8–12 mins in a 160°C oven. When they are ready, take the sticks out of the oven and keep them warm under aluminium foil.

While the meat is in the oven, put the onions, plums and strawberries in the pan used for browning the meat, fry them lightly for a minute or so and then add the strawberry wine. Cook the fruit over a gentle heat for a couple of minutes.

Take out the onions, plums and strawberries to await serving and reduce the liquid in the pan for a couple of minutes. Add a couple of spoonfuls of butter to the sauce just before serving and stir well. Check for taste and serve with the turkey shashlik and jasmine rice, for instance.

Although the epitome of a celebration meal for the Americans and many Finnish people, turkey is a low-fat, relatively mild-tasting meat. This is why the Americans put a lot of effort into the stuffing. In this case the same effect is brought about with a compôte of berries and other fruit, which is at the same time both sweet and refreshing.

BREAST OF GRAIN-FED CHICKEN WITH GINGER AND HONEY

6 tbsp honey
3–4 tbsp grated fresh ginger
1 clove of garlic, crushed
a small piece of chilli pepper, finely chopped
4 chicken breasts
rapeseed oil
4–8 pieces of vegetable marrow

Mix the honey, ginger, garlic and chilli together. Brush the chicken breasts lightly with rapeseed oil.

Grill the chicken on each side for half a minute in a really hot cast-iron pan, then brush them with the honey marinade and cook them in a 150°C oven for about 10 mins.

Cut the marrows into slices 1 cm thick and fry them in rapeseed oil until crisp and brown.

Serve with rice and salad.

Finnish chickens are some of the few that you can eat without any fear of salmonella.

REINDEER BREEDING IS AN ART!

Reindeer meat is one of the best of all the typical Finnish foodstuffs, but the way in which it is handled and processed often leaves much to be desired. Cold-smoked reindeer, for instance, has a habit of being clammy, over-salted and over-smoked, and it was certainly not a favourite of mine until I bumped into *Hannu Lahtela* in Salla.

Having studied marketing, Lahtela has become something of a guru among the new generation of meat processors in Lapland, attempting through the Best of Reindeer project and various other schemes started by individual small processing plants to standardize the regulations for handling reindeer meat, lay down a new code of quality requirements, set up systems of collaboration and develop the marketing of the meat. Hannu is involved in one way or another in almost all of these efforts.

His most important work, however, is what he does in his own processing plant, generating almost twenty good raw meat products and using the sirloin steak from reindeer calves to make excellent cold-smoked meats. For the moment these are only obtainable in Salla and in a few Helsinki restaurants, but they are bound to spread to other places in the near future.

Hannu modestly ranks himself in second place among the reindeer butchers of Lapland. Quality is the thing that matters, however, and dedication to his work.

THE FINEST REINDEER MEAT IS THAT OF A SUMMER CALF. WINTER REINDEER IS DRIER AND MORE DIFFICULT TO HANDLE, PROVIDING A REAL TEST OF THE BUTCHER'S SKILL.

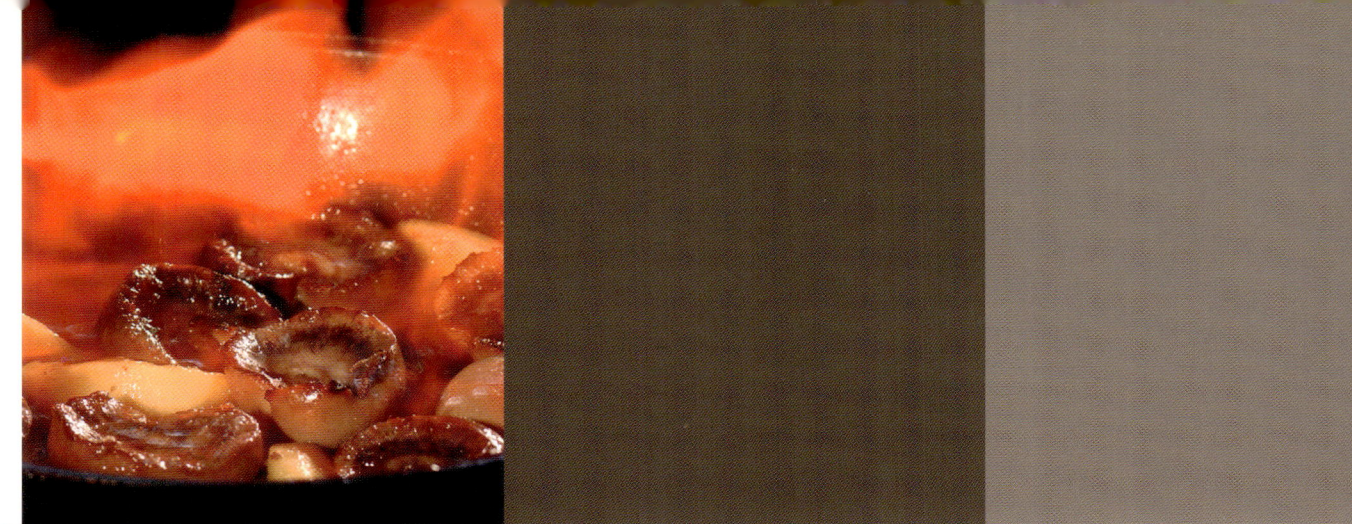

WHEN THEY HELD A FÊTE AT THE LITTLE VILLAGE OF SAIJA IN LAPLAND, HANNU LAHTELA AND I BARBEQUED REINDEER MEAT UNDER A SHELTER IN THE POURING RAIN AND SOLD AT LEAST 150 PORTIONS AT COST PRICE IN SPITE OF THE WEATHER.

THE SMALL BUT SPRIGHTLY BROWN TROUT IS ONE OF THE FINEST FISH IN LAPLAND. IT IS TRULY MAGNIFICENT COOKED OVER A CAMPFIRE AT KARHUOJA.

IT'S A WONDERFUL FEELING TO SIT BESIDE A FIRE OF PINE ROOTS ON A LIGHT SUMMER'S NIGHT, PUTTING THE WORLD TO RIGHTS AND GRILLING REINDEER LIVER ON THE END OF A STICK.

REINDEER BLOOD PANCAKES WITH SUGARED LINGONBERRIES

half an onion, finely chopped
80 g butter for frying
1 tsp anchovy juice
1 tsp marjoram
0.5 litre reindeer blood
3–4 eggs
1 bottle class I, "pilsner" beer
2 dl cream
2 dl rye flour

Cook the onion in butter with the anchovy juice and marjoram for about 15 mins. Cool and add the other ingredients. Transfer to a liquidizer and mix well for about a minute. Allow the pancake batter to rise for 20–60 mins, as fits best with your timetable.

Heat a frying pan and grease with a small knob of butter. Pour in a suitable amount of batter and fry. When the underside is suitably crisp, turn the pancake over. You can tell the right moment either by turning up the edge of the pancake or by the fact that the top surface has begun to solidify. If the temperature is right, small bubbles or holes will appear on the surface. That is the moment to turn your pancake.

Serve the pancakes with sugared crushed lingonberries and melted farmhouse butter.

If you can't get reindeer blood, pig's blood will do.

REINDEER KIDNEYS FLAMBÉS IN ÅLVADOS, WITH APPLE CREAM

16 reindeer calf kidneys
2 apples
butter and rapeseed oil for frying
3 tbsp ground green peppers
Ålvados, or calvados
6 dl whipping cream
strong mustard
salt

Remove any gristle from the kidneys and cut them in half lengthways so that you have two identical halves. Rinse them and dry them carefully. Peel the apples and cut them into segments.

Heat a frying pan and put a spoonful of oil and a spoonful of butter into it. The butter gives the kidneys better aromas and prevents the oil from becoming too hot, so that it also retains its aroma. Put the kidney halves in the pan, cut side down, fry them for a moment and turn them over. Fry them a little on the outside. Then add the apples to the pan together with the green peppers and fry quickly. Take the pan off the heat and put it on one side.

Let the kidneys cool down for a while. Then pour the spirit into the pan and set it alight – well away from the fan over the stove. If the pan is too hot the flames can be dangerous. Shake the pan well so that the kidneys are scorched on all sides.

Take the kidneys out of the pan for a moment and add the cream. Cook on the stove for a couple of minutes and then add the mustard and salt. Replace the kidneys in the sauce and allow to heat up. The kidneys are at their best, slightly pink inside, when small red drops of liquid appear on their surface. Kidneys are rather dry to eat if they are too well done.

Serve with mashed potato, boiled rice or barley.

Ålvados is an "Åland Calvados" developed there by the Tjudö Winery. Ordinary calvados will naturally do instead.

If you prefer the kidneys dry and cooked right through, cut them into thin slices at the beginning, so that they will be done completely at the frying stage.

SLOW-COOKED SHOULDER OF REINDEER CALF WITH BUTTERY MASHED POTATOES

600–800 g shoulder of reindeer calf

butter for browning

6 dl thumbnail-sized cubes of carrot, celeriac and parsnip

2 onions cut into segments

3 bay leaves

a few sprigs of rosemary and thyme, preferably fresh

8–10 juniper berries

8–10 whole black peppers

water

Dry the meat and brown it on all sides. Brown the vegetables as well.

Arrange the vegetables and half of the herbs and seasoning on the bottom of an oven dish, with the piece of meat on top, followed by the rest of the herbs and seasoning. Rinse the pan with cold water and pour this liquid over the meat. Add water so that the meat is two-thirds covered, cover the dish with a lid or piece of aluminium foil and cook in a 100°C oven for 3–4 hours or until the meat is soft and well done.

BUTTERY MASHED POTATOES:

1 kg floury potatoes, e.g. Rosamunda

2 dl full-cream milk

150 g melted butter

1/2–1 onion, grated

Boil the potatoes, pour the water off and allow them to steam until dry. Mash them in a multi-mixer or with a whisk or potato masher. Heat the milk and pour it in. Add the melted butter and stir carefully. Don't stir for too long, or the mashed potato will become heavy. Mix in the raw grated onion just before serving.

Early potatoes and fresh potatoes that have just been lifted will easily become sticky and tough if mashed. Wait a little while after the potatoes have been harvested.

REINDEER RIBS À LA HANNU LAHTELA

a row of reindeer ribs about 10 cm wide, enough for 1/2 rib per person

rapeseed oil

seasoning:
3 tbsp ground allspice
2 tbsp dried rosemary
2 tbsp chilli powder

Rub rapeseed oil into the surface of the meat with the palm of your hand. Mix the seasoning together and rub that in as well. The pieces of meat can be piled on top of each other and covered with foil.

Cook the meat in a 220°C oven for about an hour, then reduce the heat to 120° and cook for a further 4–5 hours. Cool the meat down and cut it into lengths of a couple of ribs each and brown these on the surface over a charcoal grill. The meat will heat up very quickly on the grill.

Serve with grilled onions and potatoes, for instance. A good sauce is a mayonnaise delicately flavoured with gin and juniper berries.

You can naturally make this dish with good-quality pork or lamb chops as well.

ROAST SIRLOIN OF REINDEER CALF

600–800 g boneless sirloin or tenderloin of reindeer calf

butter or rapeseed oil for browning

salt

freshly ground black peppers

Keep the joint at room temperature for a couple of hours before roasting. Put the butter or oil in a hot frying pan and brown the meat carefully on all sides. Season with salt and pepper.

Place the joint on an oven tray and roast at 140°C for about 15 mins. The temperature inside the meat should then be about 48°.

Take the joint out of the oven, wrap it in aluminium foil and allow it to stand for a while before carving. This will ensure that the juice remains inside.

Serve with halves of jacket potatoes and a mayonnaise flavoured with crushed lingonberries.

IS FINLAND BECOMING A LAND OF CHEESE?

There are lots of very tasty Finnish cheeses on the market these days, both soft farmhouse-style cheeses and hard, fermented cheeses with a downy rind that are matured lovingly for a long period and brushed regularly with salt water or alcohol, so that they develop a strong, deep taste and their flavour, aroma and character can be enjoyed to the full. I use mostly Finnish cheeses in my menus, and it is these that our overseas visitors are most interested in. Some of the cheese makers also produce traditional churned butter.

Goat's milk cheese, or chèvre, has become very fashionable recently, and many people have made the acquaintance of the Kolattu products, which range from traditional cottage cheese to goat's milk cheddar and brie. The Kolattu Dairy concentrates on cheese making and marketing nowadays, as suitable supplies of goat's milk are available from farmers in the nearby area. Cooperation is the watchword even in small-scale production. "Cooperation in marketing and transportation would help to develop this business and make it really successful," claims *Hanne Hirvonen,* an expert on Finnish cheeses, "It's just that it's sometimes so very difficult for the Finns."

The "Flying Cow" cheese stall run by the Hirvonen sisters in Hakaniemi Market Hall in Helsinki has specialized in Finnish cheeses. It stocks about 30 of these, which account for some 40 per cent of its total sales. The stall has good cold storage facilities capable of holding the products of numerous small cheese factories, and it is through this outlet that I usually find it most convenient to buy my cheeses.

The problem for small cheese makers in Finland, for all their reliance on quality, is the sparse and inadequate nature of the sales network. It is difficult to break into the big chains of food stores in a profitable fashion, so that small, private shops offer the best opportunity. There are only a dozen or so market halls left in the country, however, and it is essential that people frequent these and demand that they should be supported in every way possible. Otherwise an essential part of our food culture is likely to disappear.

FINNISH GOAT'S MILK CHEESES ARE SLIGHTLY SWEETER THAN THOSE PRODUCED IN THE GREAT CHEESE COUNTRIES OF THE WORLD. SOME PEOPLE ARE PUT OFF BY THIS, BUT OTHERS FIND IT ESPECIALLY ATTRACTIVE.

THE AMOUNT OF CHEESE AVAILABLE IN THE SHOPS HAS INCREASED GREATLY SINCE WE JOINED THE EU. THE POPULARITY OF WINE DRINKING HAS STIMULATED SALES OF CHEESE AS WELL, AND A GENUINE INTEREST HAS BEEN AROUSED IN LOCAL FINNISH CHEESES, WHICH SHOULD DEFINITELY BE ACCOMPANIED BY THE PRODUCTS OF LOCAL WINERIES.

THE KOLATTU DAIRY IN SOMERO IS ONE OF THE BEST-KNOWN PRODUCERS OF GOAT'S MILK CHEESE IN FINLAND. MANY PEOPLE ARE FAMILIAR WITH ITS TRADITIONAL COTTAGE CHEESE, GOAT'S MILK CHEDDAR, BRIE AND FETA AND HERB FETA, WHICH THEY CAN FIND IN THEIR OWN FOOD SHOPS.

REMEMBER TO KEEP CHEESE AT ROOM TEMPERATURE FOR A FEW HOURS BEFORE SERVING, TO BRING OUT ITS FULL FLAVOUR AND AROMA.

CHEESE IS MADE BY ADDING RENNET TO THE MILK AT JUST THE RIGHT TEMPERATURE AND STIRRING THE CURDS TO OBTAIN THE DESIRED TEXTURE.

MODERN CELLARS FOR RIPENING CHEESE IMITATE CONDITIONS IN THE TRADITIONAL NATURAL CELLARS OR CAVES. THE AROMA IS OFTEN QUITE UNBELIEVABLE!
AN IMPORTANT PART OF THE PROCESS FOR MANY CHEESES IS REPEATED BRUSHING OF THE OUTER CRUST WITH BRINE OR ALCOHOL, SOMETIMES EVEN RED WINE OR BRANDY.

BRIE SOUP AND FRIED BRIE

2 shallots

a piece of carrot

a piece of celeriac

100 g mushrooms (champignons)

butter for frying

1 litre pale meat stock

1 dl demi-sec white wine

1 sprig each of thyme and parsley

200 g brie cheese

3 dl cream

2 dl beer

Cut up the vegetables and fry them lightly in butter with the mushrooms for a couple of minutes. Then cover them with a lid and allow them to sweat for a while.

Add the meat stock, wine and herbs, cook for about 15 mins and strain. Add the cheese and cook until it has all dissolved. Add the cream, bring to the boil and flavour with the beer.

The Finnish Mäkiaho Brie is excellent for this soup, and I prefer to add the Laitila Brewery's Kukko beer at the end. This is also suitable for serving with the soup.

FRIED GOAT'S MILK BRIE:

1 dl finely chopped herbs: parsley, chervil and a few leaves of thyme

1 dl fresh breadcrumbs

2 eggs

a piece of goat's milk brie (about 50 g) per person

flour

butter and rapeseed oil

1 clove of garlic, chopped

Mix the herbs with the breadcrumbs, whip the eggs and dilute with a drop of water. Dip the pieces of cheese first in the flour, then in the egg and finally in the breadcrumbs and herbs. Fry them in a mixture of butter and oil with a little garlic added.

Serve with the brie soup.

FRIED CHEESE WITH APPLE PURÉE

2 cooking apples
0.5 dl sugar
a piece of vanilla pod
a piece of cinnamon pod
300–400 g Werneri goat's milk brie
butter for frying

Cut the apples into pieces, cook them to a pulp with the sugar, vanilla pod and cinnamon, and cool.

Cut the cheese into suitable-sized pieces and fry these quickly in the butter or warm them in a hot oven. Arrange them on a serving plate with the apple purée as a sauce.

There are a number of good Finnish goat's milk cheeses that are excellent for frying in this way, but I prefer the very popular, slightly harder Werneri brie from the Kolattu Dairy. It has just the right thickness of rind for this purpose and a splendid taste. It is also delicious for breakfast when grilled and served with a sweet jam.

EVERY LOAF OF BREAD IS WORTH A SONG

Imagine the enchanting smell of loaves of rye bread from fourteen small bakeries set out side by side on one table. I was one of those privileged to be present when an enthusiastic jury of connoisseurs set about evaluating the aroma of these loaves, their browned and slightly cracked crusts, the soft texture of the bread inside and other essential properties.

The traditional Finnish rye bread loaf is a national treasure that should be preserved at all costs. This would also mean the continued cultivation of rye in this country and to a great extent the retention of the main aspect of the work of hundreds of small bakeries.

Elvi Avikainen still shapes the loaves of her own rye bread in what must be the last small bakery to function in the basement of a house in Helsinki. She has been doing this work in the Sörnäinen district of the city for virtually fifty years. Meanwhile her daughter puts the finishing touches to a delicious-looking sandwich loaf – these have become very popular again – and her son sets out to deliver their products to a clientele of small shops.

Emil Halme's bakery at Kauklahti in Espoo has been going strong for 105 years now. This is a medium-sized enterprise with 22 employees, producing black rye bread, Gotland bread, ordinary rye bread baked in a stone oven and many other traditional items. The fourth generation of bakers is about to take over responsibility for keeping up these traditions.

There are still more 800 small bakeries in Finland. The bakers grow old in their time, but Finnish bread lives on. Where else in the world will you find such a variety of fine traditional forms of bread?

FINNISH BREAD IS FAR MORE THAN JUST RYE BREAD. TAKE THE FINE MALT BREADS OF THE COASTAL AREA AND ARCHIPELAGO, FOR INSTANCE, AS PRODUCED AT MALAX, AT ROSALA ON THE ISLAND OF HITIS, AT EKENÄS AND AT HANKO.

THE BLACK BREAD OF ÅLAND IS FLAT, FIRM AND HEAVY, AND KEEPS WELL. CONTRARY TO WHAT PEOPLE IMAGINE, THE BLACK COLOUR DOES NOT COME FROM BLOOD BUT FROM THE RYE FLOUR AND THE LONG BAKING TIME. OTHER SECRETS OF ITS EXCELLENT FLAVOUR ARE THE USE OF MALT AND SYRUP, AND IN SOME CASES BRUSHING OF THE NEWLY BAKED LOAVES WITH BEER.

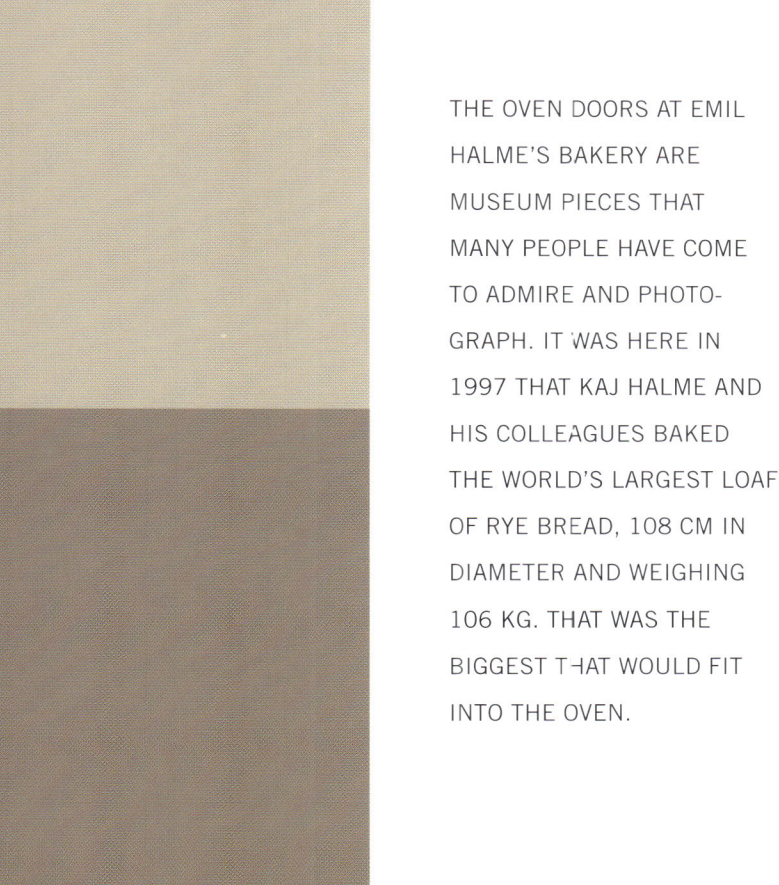

THE OVEN DOORS AT EMIL HALME'S BAKERY ARE MUSEUM PIECES THAT MANY PEOPLE HAVE COME TO ADMIRE AND PHOTOGRAPH. IT WAS HERE IN 1997 THAT KAJ HALME AND HIS COLLEAGUES BAKED THE WORLD'S LARGEST LOAF OF RYE BREAD, 108 CM IN DIAMETER AND WEIGHING 106 KG. THAT WAS THE BIGGEST THAT WOULD FIT INTO THE OVEN.

A RESTAURANT'S BREAD BASKET IS ONE OF ITS BEST RECOMMENDATIONS. PERHAPS FOR THIS REASON, MANY FINNISH RESTAURANTS BAKE THEIR OWN BREAD, SOME OF THEM TWICE A DAY.

THE ILMATAR RESTAURANT'S CLERK

25 g yeast
16 g salt
5 dl water, at room temperature
450 g plain bread flour
150 g wheat flour

Mix the ingredients together, first the yeast and salt, then the flour. Knead with a universal mixer for about ten minutes until the dough is of a suitable consistency, put it on one side to rise for about 45 mins and then knead at few times again.

Cut the dough into suitable-sized pieces and form them into loaves. Place these on a floured cloth to rise for about one and a half hours. Use the cloth to move the loaves onto an oven tray covered with greaseproof paper and put the tray in the oven.

Bake for about 15 mins at 220°C and then for 40 mins at 200°C.

To get a crisp crust on the bread, put a little water in a small cup in the oven at the same time.

The name Clerk refers to a recipe obtained from an Austrian baker. In our restaurant we make it out of bread flour from Kemiö that is generally available at retail and wholesale outlets. It has no additives whatsoever and is of a good gluten strength.

UNLEAVENED BARLEY BREAD 1 AND 2

UNLEAVENED
BARLEY BREAD 1:

1 kg barley flour

1 tsp salt

3.5 dl water

3.5 dl Finnish soured milk, piimä

1 tsp baking soda

Mix all the ingredients together to form a dough. Divide this dough into four parts and roll each out together with some flour to a thickness of just under a centimetre. Prick with a fork on both sides. Bake in a 250°C oven.

UNLEAVENED
BARLEY BREAD 2:

1 kg barley flour

5 dl water

4 dl milk

1 dl sour cream

1 tsp baking soda

1 tsp salt

Mix all the ingredients together to form a dough. Divide this dough into four parts and roll each out to a thickness of just under a centimetre. Prick with a fork on both sides. Bake at 250°C.

COMB PASTRIES

(to make about 20 pastries)

250 g butter
1.5 dl sugar
0.5 tsp baking soda
200 g Finnish fermented milk, viili
1 egg
750 g flour

Mix the butter (kept at room temperature) and sugar together in a bowl. Stir the soda into the fermented milk and combine them immediately with the butter and sugar mixture. Add the egg and flour and mix to an even dough.

Roll the dough out into a rectangular slab, using plenty of flour to prevent it from sticking.

Put the dough in a cool place to harden for a while, then cut it into 4 x 8 cm pieces and make 3–5 cuts in each so that they look like wide-toothed combs. Bake for 5–10 mins in a 270°C oven.

It is also possible to make savoury comb pastries. The traditional number of teeth in the comb varies somewhat from place to place within Finland.

WINE FROM FINLAND? OF COURSE.

Let's stop off on our journey at Laitikkala near Hämeenlinna for a glass of wine. The spacious farmyard of Rönnvik with its red-brick buildings is like a postcard, and the café-restaurant and wine shop are teeming with visitors. The fields all around us contain more than 100,000 currant bushes, and the farm's own picking machine is working away busily, gathering the ripe berries and cleaning them ready for processing.

Winemaking began at Rönnvik in 1995, and the modern production facilities here, from the freezing plant to the juice presses and fermentation vessels, represent the latest technology.

Rönnvik has deservedly won prizes as Winery of the Year, and its range of wines has now been supplemented with three high quality varieties of spirit with just a whiff of currant about them.

At Ranua in the north of the country we find a winery of a different kind. Behind the stylish retail shop is the only winery in the country that relies entirely on wild berries. Here the juice from frozen crowberries, lingonberries and other highlights of nature in the north mature in thousand-litre tanks to yield delicate wines that are then sold in custom-designed bottles and gift wraps. The wine-makers, *Terttu* and *Oiva Nurmela,* emphasize that here, too, quality is the key to success.

The bus-loads of visitors to Ranua are naturally the main customers for the Northern Lights Winery. "It's only a pity that we're not allowed to sell them our equally fine liqueurs," Oiva Nurmela complains.

I myself try to serve local Finnish berry wines with my meals whenever I can, as a change from our usual fine range of conventional wines.

IN MARKUS' OPINION

The Finnish local wines are produced entirely from Finnish berries and fruit, mostly grown on the same farm, and have a maximum alcohol content of 13 per cent.

I had my real introduction to local wines when I did my final dissertation on this topic at the Turku Vocational Institute, although I had been interested in them earlier and was already convinced that people in Finland did not appreciate them as they should.

There are almost 50 registered local wineries in the country nowadays, and expertise in wine making is being developed all the time, partly through courses at the Muuruvesi Wine Information Centre and at Lepaa, where some excellent wines are also made.

I have sometimes been a judge at the Local Wine of the Year competitions. The standard varies, naturally, but the majority of the wines are really good and the best quite exceptional.

Although local wineries nowadays are able to rely on research findings and advanced technology, the basic method remains the same as ever. The juice is extracted from pre-frozen berries, sugar and well water are added and the must is fermented with yeast in huge stainless steel vats, allowed to mature, filtered and bottled. Finally it is stored in cellars until it is ready to be sold and enjoyed.

A little while ago a quality system was devised for fruit and berry wines that takes account of all the significant characteristics of a wine: external appearance, bouquet and flavour – the combination that is so crucial to the wine taster. Bottles produced by local Finnish wineries in 2005 have quality markings on them in accordance with this system.

We once sent a bottle of Bothnia Plain crowberry wine to Burgundy for the connoisseurs there to taste, and in the first blind tasting they thought it was an Italian red wine. In actual fact one should not try to compare berry wines with grape-based wines at all. They form a category of their own and should be evaluated as such. Unfortunately many people in Finland still feel a certain prejudice against them, which is quite unnecessary.

I also believe there is a case for allowing local wines to be sold in the food shops and fortified wines directly at the wineries. At present the law in Finland permits the direct sale of table wines at the wineries (subject to licence) but stronger wines, liqueurs etc. can only be sold by the national alcoholic beverages monopoly.

LET'S HAVE A QUICK BEER

A small local brewery is defined in Finland as one that produces at the most 10 million litres of beer a year.

The fashion for small breweries began with the commercial revival of the traditional Finnish peasant beer sahti by a company in Lammi in 1987, and its manager, *Pekka Kääriänen,* is still one of the leading figures in this line of business. Altogether there are just under 20 small local breweries operating in this country at present, with their own Brewers' Association, beer festivals, enthusiastic devotees and consumers' magazines.

Let's go along to the Punavuori area near the centre of Helsinki for a quick glass of beer. The Iloinen Lohi (Happy Salmon) bar stocks an enormous range of beers, bottled or on draught, including many from small Finnish breweries. Maybe we should order the variety brewed specially for this bar by the Stadi brewery, based in the city itself, as the name implies. Many small breweries produce beers specifically for sale on draught at certain bars, and quite a number have a beer restaurant of their own as their principal outlet.

Under a recent reform of the alcoholic beverages tax, small breweries were granted tax concessions of between five and ten percent depending on their production figures. If only they could be granted a licence to sell beer for taking off the premises, and if only the state liquor monopoly would agree to stock more of their products, their situation would look quite promising.

Supporters of the small breweries are of the opinion that the best of them produce beers that are in a class of their own. The sahti from Lammi, for instance, has nothing whatsoever to do with the home-brewed stuff of the same name that used to upset your stomach and give you a headache in earlier times. *Michael Jackson,* perhaps the world's best-known beer guru, was delighted with it.

FLAVOURS, FIBRES AND FLAVONOIDS

I use Finnish fruit and berries in most of my desserts. The Finns love these flavours which they have been used to from their childhood and visitors admire their fresh taste.

It is also said that they are infinitely more healthy than imported fruit. Finnish apples, for instance, have large amounts of flavinoids in them, which apparently prevent both cancer and cardiovascular diseases.

And these are delicacies that are non-fattening. A medium-sized apple contains only 37 kilocalories (155 kJ), about half the energy that there is in a sandwich biscuit. Research has also shown that berries prevent the growth of harmful intestinal bacteria.

One of our leading health experts, *Prof. Pekka Puska,* has said that Finnish berries are in many respects a preferable alternative to imported fruit. They are clean, light and contain large amounts of fibre, vitamins, anti-oxidants and other valuable substances.

But a kitchen is not supposed to be a pharmacy. A dessert can sometimes be a sinful act of hedonism, with no thought for the calories. I like to put a good dash of cream and sugar in my desserts on occasions, but if raspberry or apple has a heavenly taste, then why shouldn't it be healthy as well?

The desserts described here can be served with sweet local berry wines or the corresponding liqueurs.

RHUBARB SLIPPER WITH VANILLA SAUCE

puff pastry, home-made or frozen

1 dl sugar

1 egg for brushing

3 tbsp ground cinnamon

12–16 sticks of rhubarb, cut into 10 cm pieces

Roll out the pastry to a thickness of about 0.5 cm and cut out circles of diameter 8–10 cm. Spread the working surface with sugar and place the circles on top of the sugar. Roll them out gently from the centre in two opposing directions, leaving the ends slightly thicker. Brush lightly with egg and sprinkle with a little sugar and cinnamon.

Pile 4–8 pieces of rhubarb on each piece of pastry and cook in a 225°C oven for about 15 mins. When both the rhubarb and the pastry are done the pastry should turn up at the ends like the sole of an old shoe.

Serve with vanilla sauce.

VANILLA SAUCE:

1 vanilla pod

3 dl whipping cream

2 dl milk

6 egg yolks

150 g sugar

Split the vanilla pod down the centre and put both halves in the milk. Heat gently for about 10 mins.

Whip the egg yolks and sugar to a froth, pour in the cream and milk and stir well. Return the mixture to the saucepan and thicken it gradually over a water bath.

Use the "rose test" to see when the sauce is ready: dip a spoon into the sauce and bring it out upside down. Blow gently on the convex surface of the upturned spoon. When the liquid on it forms a rose pattern the sauce is done.

Take the saucepan out of the water bath and cool it in iced water. Serve the vanilla sauce with the hot rhubarb slippers.

FROZEN CRANBERRIES AND HOT TOFFEE SAUCE

1.5 dl ice-cold cranberries per person
icing sugar

Sprinkle plenty of icing sugar on the cranberries.

TOFFEE SAUCE:
5 dl whipping cream
1 dl milk
4 dl sugar

Put all the ingredients in a saucepan and allow to boil gently until the mixture is suitably thick.

FRESH STRAWBERRIES AND STRAWBERRY ZABAGLIONE

SYRUP FOR MARINADING THE STRAWBERRIES:

2 dl water

140 g sugar

a piece of star anise

half a vanilla pod

a piece of cinnamon stick

a piece each of lemon and orange rind

1 litre strawberries

Combine all the ingredients for the marinade, cook on a gentle heat for a couple of minutes and cool.

Pour the syrup onto the strawberries through a strainer. They don't have to be covered. It is enough if they are more or less in contact with the marinade. Lift them gently and stir them about.

ZABAGLIONE:

6 egg yolks

1.5 dl strawberry wine

100 g sugar

Mix the ingredients together and thicken to a well-cooked foam over a water bath, stirring vigorously. Whip further until the foam is cold.

Serve the strawberries out into fairly deep dishes and pour a generous portion of the zabaglione on top of each dish to cover the strawberries completely.

BAKED APPLES WITH AN OAT-FLAKE CRUST

6–10 autumn apples
lemon juice
1–2 tbsp butter
3–4 tbsp sugar
1–1.5 dl oat flakes
2 dl whipping cream

Peel the apples, cut them into slices about 0.5 cm thick and moisten these with lemon juice. Arrange the slices elegantly in a dish greased with butter.

Put a spoonful of butter in a warm pan and add the sugar. Allow the sugar to melt and turn slightly brown. Then add the oat flakes and cream. Bring to the boil and pour over the apples. Heat in a 220°C oven for 10–15 mins so that the apples cook.

This dish is wonderful with ice-cream.

QUARK AND LEMON CREAM WITH A SPELT BISCUIT

18–20 g sheet gelatine
6 yolks of free-range eggs
190 g sugar
1 dl lemon juice
3 dl milk
4 dl cream
1 dl quark

First put the gelatine into a large volume of cold water to soak. Whip the egg yolks with 140 g of the sugar. Then bring the lemon juice to the boil with the remaining 50 g of sugar.

Combine the egg yolks with the milk and thicken over a water bath on the stove. Dip the convex side of a wooden spoon in the mixture and blow on it. When a rose pattern appears, i.e. there are waves on it, it is done sufficiently. Take the bowl out of the water bath and add the lemon juice after it has come to the boil. Save a couple of spoonfuls of the juice for dissolving the gelatine.

Whip the cream to a froth. Cool the mixture of milk, egg and lemon juice and add the quark. At this point squeeze the water out of the gelatine and heat the sheets gently in the remaining lemon juice. Fold the gelatine quickly into the mixture, whisking vigorously, and immediately afterwards add the cream. Serve out into dishes rinsed in cold water and put in the cold to set.

A thickened and sweetened sauce of sea buckthorn berries, made more or less in the manner of a fruit compôte, is ideal with this cream.

SPELT BISCUITS:
50 g melted butter
60 g spelt flakes
1.5 dl sugar
1 egg
1 tbsp flour
1 tsp baking powder

Mix all the ingredients together. Allow to settle for a moment.

Measure out little heaps of the mixture onto an oven tray and flatten them slightly with a spatula. Bake in a 225°C oven for about 5 mins, until done.

Many of these recipes refer to free-range eggs. When you find a small chicken farm in the country that sells free-range eggs, make the most of it. I have for a long time been buying most of mine from Mika Rasilainen, a farmer in Somero.

FROZEN SEA BUCKTHORN SOUFFLÉ WITH BLACKCURRANT PURÉE

ITALIAN MERINGUE:

150 g sugar

1.5 dl water

2 tbsp juice of sea buckthorn berries

Combine all the ingredients and heat to about 120°C. If you have no thermometer, twist a paper-clip into a loop and dip it in the sugar. If a distinct film forms across the loop the sugar has reached 120°C.

2 egg whites

80 g sugar

Whip the egg whites and sugar to a stiff froth and pour the sugared sea buckthorn juice into it carefully in a thin stream. Whip the meringue until it has cooled down.

3 dl cream

80 g sugar

Combine the cream and sugar and whip to a fairly stiff foam.

8 egg yolks

1 dl sea buckthorn liqueur

1.5 dl juice of sea buckthorn berries

150 g sugar

Combine all these ingredients and thicken over a water bath to form a cooked, foamy mixture. Allow this to cool and fold it carefully into the meringue. Add the whipped cream last.

Insert rings of greaseproof paper around the inside of the desired number of coffee cups, projecting a few centimetres above the rim, and fill the cups and paper rings with the mixture. Put the cups into a freezer until the mixture is solid. Take the papers off before serving.

This soufflé can be served with sugared blackcurrant sauce, for instance.

I often flavour my blackcurrant sauce with redcurrant sparkling wine from B. W. Heikel, a fruit grower in Lepaa.

SMALL PANCAKES WITH VANILLA CRÈME AND WILD STRAWBERRY JAM

PANCAKE BATTER:

4 dl full-cream milk
2 eggs
just under 1 dl pancake flour
1 tsp sugar
grated rind of half a lemon
50 g melted butter

Mix all the ingredients together in a liquidizer and allow to rise for at least two hours. Form the batter into small pancakes and fry them.

VANILLA CRÈME:

1 vanilla pod
0.5 litre full-cream milk
150 g sugar
6 egg yolks
80 g cornflour or barley thickening

Split the vanilla pod in two lengthways, put it into the milk and allow it to stand on a gentle heat for 15 mins. Whip the sugar and egg yolks to a froth and stir in the cornflower. Add the milk to this froth and thicken on the stove, stirring constantly, preferably with a wooden spoon.

The mixture is ready when it is really thick. Then squeeze it through a sieve and mix in a knob of butter. Spread this crème on the pancakes and build them up into a pile.

Serve with jam made of wild strawberries if at all possible, or else with ordinary strawberry jam.

THE STARS OF THIS BOOK

Magnus Koskinen
strawberry and asparagus grower, Sibbo
My local supplier of green asparagus, the great strength of which lies in its absolute freshness.

Juhani Hirvonen
potato farmer, Ylämylly, Liperi
A tireless product developer and my collaborator in all matters concerning potatoes. We have tested many varieties together, and it is thanks to him that I now know more about potatoes than I used to.

Ville Holopainen
lettuce grower, Kirkkonummi
Holopainen's market garden with its dozens of varieties of lettuce is not far away, and he will have picked them only a few hours before they reach me. This is a family business which strives for quality rather than huge volumes.

Esa Lahtinen
Uusikaupunki
The firm Esa runs with Pekka Vapanen, Kalaset Oy, is no longer a small enterprise. It now provides work for a host of local fishermen and small fish farms, all committed to the same high standards of quality.

Kalle and Paula Piipanoja
Nagu
The Piipanoja Company must have won all the prizes for quality that it is possible to win in their line of business in Finland, and a good number of diplomas from abroad as well. My favourite is their cold-smoked Baltic herring, but their cold-smoked salmon is the product that has made it to the shops in some places.

Virpi and Antti Rantalainen
Hauhala goose farm, Anttola
Pioneers of goose farming and marketing of the products. This is a good example of inheriting a farm and boldly changing its line of production to something utterly original.

Outi Kolattu-Tolvi and Janne Tolvi
Kolattu goat cheese dairy, Somero
Goat cheese is one of the tastiest of the recent innovations in Finnish food products, and the Kolattu cheeses have already reached the best food shops and delicatessens. The picture is of Janne Tolvi.

Eila and Ismo Eerola
Heikkola piggery and Benjamin's Country Market, Kausala
The Eerolas raise pork that is tender and flavoursome, and an equally commendable business is Eila's country market, which gathers together all the best local produce from their area, from potatoes to rye bread.

Hannu Lahtela
The Wild Reindeer, Salla
Lahtela does valuable work both as a businessman in the village of Salla and as an active representative of the producers of reindeer meat and those eager to establish a quality system for it.

Eila and Jouni Rönni
Rönnvik fruit farm, Laitikkala
Rönnvik has won the Winery of the Year award in Finland on many occasions. This estate in southern Häme with its idyllic farm buildings, huge fields of currant bushes, modern winemaking facilities, stylish wine shop and a café-restaurant of its own is an impressive place to visit.

Sebastian and Ûlle Nurmi
Bovik organic sheep farm, Snappertuna
The meat from Bovik's Finnish sheep has won a prize as the best food ingredient in the country, and the farm has gained a great deal of publicity. The sheep also do a lot of good landscaping work in the summer. The picture shows Ûlle with one of the sheepdogs.

Hanne and Laura Hirvonen
The Flying Cow cheese stall,
Hakaniemi Market Hall, Helsinki
About a fifth of the stall's merchandise is Finnish – and more than a half of their sales income comes from Finnish cheeses. A unique place for all cheese lovers in the Helsinki area.

Terttu and Oiva Nurmela
Ranua Northern Lights Ltd
The Nurmelas have been making wines, liqueurs, jellies and juices from a selection of wild berries from the north ranging from cloudberries to crowberries since 1998.

INDEX

Ålvados, for reindeer
kidney flambé 115
Anchovies, with baked Baltic
herrings and mashed potato 55
Apples, baked, with an
oat-flake crust 155
Asparagus, country butter sauce
and belly of pork 25
Asparagus marinaded in orange
oil, with virgin salad 21
Asparagus salad with
oven-dried tomatoes 22
Baked apples with an
oat-flake crust 55
Baked Baltic herrings with
anchovies and mashed potato 55
Baltic herring tartare with
beetroot jelly 51
Baltic herrings, baked, with
anchovies and mashed potato 55
Barley bread, unleavened, 1 137
Barley bread, unleavened, 2 137
Barley risotto 80
Beetroot cooked in orange juice 57
Beetroot jelly 51
Beetroot timbale with
lingonberry sauce and ceps 38
Beetroots baked in the oven,
with goat cheese sauce 37
Belly of pork stuffed with fruit 76

Belly of pork, with asparagus
and country butter sauce 25
Belly of pork, with chanterelles
and poached egg 26
Black soup 102
Blackcurrant purée 159
Blood pancakes, reindeer,
with sugared lingonberries 113
Boiled red cabbage 97
Breast of duck with rhubarb sauce 99
Breast of grain-fed chicken
with ginger and honey 107
Brie, goat's milk, fried 129
Brie soup and fried goat's milk brie ..126
Buttery mashed potatoes 117
Carelian stew à la Markus 79
Carrot, creamed 74
Ceps, with beetroot timbale
and lingonberry sauce 38
Chanterelles, poached egg
and belly of pork 26
Chanterelles, sautéed 61
Chanterelles with charr shashlik 61
Charr shashlik with chanterelles 61
Cherry tomato and onion salad 91
Chicken breast with ginger
and honey 107
Clerk, from the Ilmatar Restaurant ...134
Cold-smoked Baltic herring
tartare with beetroot jelly 51

Comb pastries 139
Country butter sauce 25
Crayfish soup with Skagen salad 52
Creamed carrot 74
Cucumber and whitefish
roe in sorrel sauce 17
Dill and cream sauce 65
Dill in smetana 31
Duck breast with rhubarb sauce 99
Duck, wild, traditional casserole 97
Fresh strawberries and
strawberry zabaglione 152
Fried goat's milk brie 129
Fried Ohtakari whitefish with
beetroot cooked in orange juice 57
Frozen cranberries and
hot toffee sauce 151
Frozen sea buckthorn soufflé
with blackcurrant purée 159
Game and cream sauce 97
Glassmaster's rainbow trout 46
Goat cheese sauce 37
Goat's milk brie, fried 126
Goose, roast, for St. Martin's Day 101
Ham, sauna-cured 74
Herring caviar 32
Hirvonen's black potatoes 34
Ilmatar Restaurant's Clerk 134
Lamb and cabbage rolls 93

Leeks au gratin, with
goat cheese sauce 19
Lemon and qark cream
with a spelt biscuit 157
Lieksa turnip soup 40
Lingonberries, sugared,
with reindeer blood pancakes...........113
Lingonberry sauce............................38
Markus the Chef's
pork sausage soup 82
Minced meat steak with
sauna-cured ham 74
Nettle sauce......................................17
New potatoes, vendace roe
and dill in smetana 31
Oat-flake crust................................155
Orange oil marinade........................21
Organical minced meat steak
with sauna-cured ham......................74
Oven-dried tomatoes........................22
Ox-tail and barley risotto 80
Pancakes with vanilla crème
and wild strawberry jam..................160
Pike laced with anchovy in
a dill and cream sauce 65
Pike poached in cooling stock,
with browned horseradish butter.........69
Pike quenelles with nettle sauce 67
Poached egg 26
Poached pike with
browned horseradish butter...............69

Pork sausage soup 82
Potato pancake and herring caviar......32
Quark and lemon cream
with a spelt biscuit 157
Red cabbage, boiled 97
Reindeer blood pancakes
with sugared lingonberries...............113
Reindeer calf, roast sirloin...............121
Reindeer kidneys flambés
in Ålvados, with apple cream 115
Reindeer ribs à la Hannu Lahtela 119
Rhubarb slipper with vanilla sauce ...149
Ribs of reindeer à la
Hannu Lahtela 119
Roach tartare à la Juha Niemiö 49
Roast goose for St. Martin's Day.......101
Roast sirloin of reindeer calf 121
St. Martin's Day roast goose...........101
Salmon and potato casserole
à la Markus 62
Sauna-cured ham 74
Sautéed chanterelles........................61
Sea buckthorn soufflé,
with blackcurrant purée..................159
Shashlik of charr with chanterelles.....61
Shoulder of lamb cooked in foil..........89
Skagen salad....................................52
Sirloin of reindeer calf, roast...........121
Slow-cooked shoulder of reindeer calf
with buttery mashed potatoes 117

Slowly cooked shank of lamb
with cherry tomato and onion salad 91
Small pancakes with vanilla crème
and wild strawberry jam..................160
Sorrel sauce......................................17
Sour cream sauce 34
Spelt biscuits.................................157
Strawberries and
strawberry zabaglione....................152
Strawberry zabaglione 152
Toffee sauce...................................151
Traditional wild duck casserole..........97
Turkey shashlik with
warm fruit compote........................105
Turnip soup Ninon from Lieksa...........40
Unleavened barley bread 1 137
Unleavened barley bread 2 137
Vanilla crème 160
Vanilla sauce..................................149
Vendace roe, new potatoes
and dill in smetana...........................31
Virgin salad 21
Whitefish, fried, with beetroot
cooked in orange juice 57
Whitefish roe and cucumber
in sorrel sauce..................................17
Wild duck casserole, traditional..........97
Wild strawberry jam 160
Young pike laced with anchovy
in a dill and cream sauce 65
Zabaglione, strawberry 152

PARTICULAR THANKS GO TO

The authors' long-suffering families

E. Eriksson, wholesale fishmongers

Mirja Hellstedt, Finnfood

Rein Meats Ltd

Royal Restaurants Ltd

Pekka Väisänen, Ministry of Agriculture and Forestry

Soili Jääskeläinen, Otava

The many producers and processors of foodstuffs who have helped in the making of this book

The Quality Chain and its 22 links

The many friends and connoisseurs who have encouraged and advised us when we have given them a hint of what were doing.